TERROR IN VIET NAM

Other books by Jay Mallin

FORTRESS CUBA

CARIBBEAN CRISIS

TERROR IN

VIET NAM

by

JAY MALLIN

D. VAN NOSTRAND COMPANY, INC.

Princeton, New Jersey

Toronto   *New York*   *London*

D. VAN NOSTRAND COMPANY, INC.
120 Alexander St., Princeton, New Jersey (*Principal office*)
24 West 40 Street, New York 18, New York

D. VAN NOSTRAND COMPANY, LTD.
358, Kensington High Street, London, W.14, England
D. VAN NOSTRAND COMPANY (*Canada*), LTD.
25 Hollinger Road, Toronto 16

First published May 1966
Reprinted November 1966

PRINTED IN THE UNITED STATES OF AMERICA

TO MOTHER AND DAD

CONTENTS

INTRODUCTION

"I am always worried about my fate." Tran Van Hoa, Chief of Tan My Chanh hamlet, smiled grimly as he spoke. From the bare, bullet-scarred building which serves as his headquarters, I could see the barbed wire, earthworks and local forces guards that give a slight measure of protection from the unseen Viet Cong forces in the surrounding rice paddies and jungle. The chief, thirty-four years old and the father of six children, said: "A construction man in this hamlet was beheaded by the VC [Viet Cong]. The police chief was killed. The VC put a mine in front of my house. Three times the VC have entered the hamlet." "Yes," said Tran Van Hoa, "I am always worried about my fate."

The My Canh floating restaurant in Saigon was a colorful place the evening of June 25, 1965, illuminated by lanterns and multi-hued lights, full, but not crowded, with some one hundred diners. It was a pleasant evening, cool and clear. At 8:15 P.M., a white flash lit the area; there was a deafening explosion and pellets and fragments sprayed the diners with deadly effect. The lights went out. There were moans and sharp screams,

and the dead were everywhere. Frightened survivors
scurried to cover, while the braver sought in the dark-
ness to help the wounded.

Terror is a weapon as real, and sometimes more
deadly than a gun. For it can kill not only the
body, but the spirit of those lives it touches with
fear. It sets friend against friend, family against
family, and even children against parents. It never
warns in advance, but strikes at any time with a
variety of means.

To the Communists, terror is not a casual cir-
cumstance of war. Rather it is a highly-developed,
highly-refined political weapon designed to fester
unseen from within, soften resistance to the enemy
that *can* be seen, and set the stage for complete
collapse of the target against which it is directed.
Once in power, the Communists have used it
routinely to control their own people.

Violence has always played an integral part of
Communist theory. In 1905, Lenin declared,
"The revolutionary army is needed because great
historical questions can be solved only by violence
and the organization in the modern struggle is a
military organization."

If Lenin thus made terror official policy, Stalin
and Mao Tse-tung perfected it as an instrument
for gaining and consolidating power. Khrushchev
himself revealed Stalin's uses of terror in his
famous speech to the Twentieth Soviet Party Con-

gress, and Mao Tse-tung piously said, "Let a hundred flowers bloom," only to lop off the blossoms of dissent that conveniently, if innocently, made themselves known.

More recently, Ho Chi Minh in North Vietnam and Fidel Castro in Cuba have applied it as dutiful students to bring Communist minority elements of revolutionary movements into positions of dominance. Said Castro's theoretician, Ernesto Guevara, "We should not fear violence, the midwife of new societies; but that violence should solely be unleashed . . . at the precise moment in which the leaders of the people [i.e. the Communist chiefs] have found the circumstances to be most favorable."

This book seeks to provide a journalist's up-to-the-minute picture of the Communist "science" of terror as it is being applied in South Viet Nam today. In the Caribbean, I saw the tactic used successfully in Cuba and I saw it thwarted in the Dominican Republic. My report of this latest application is based on this Caribbean experience, first-hand observation in Vietnamese hamlets and Saigon, and talks with South Vietnamese officials and civilians and United States military and civilian advisors.

Words such as "strategy," "theory," and "tactics" have something of the armchair abstract about them, while the life of Tran Van Hoa at Tan My Chanh and the lives of customers and employees at the bombed-out My Canh restaurant in Saigon do not. It is hoped that, for the reader of this book, Communist theory will take on the reality of flesh and, most appallingly, blood that it is for the citizens of South Viet Nam.

JAY MALLIN

Coral Gables, Florida
February, 1966

Chapter I

STAGE FOR TERROR

"The history of Viet Nam began, according to popular legend, more than four thousand years ago on a beautiful morning when Kin De Minh, a descendant of the Chinese King Than Nong, went on a tour to the south and met at Ngu Linh Mountains, Ho Nam Province, a fairy whom he married and who bore him a son by the name of Loc Tuc.

"Loc Tuc received from his father the southern part of his kingdom, and he reigned there under the name of Kinh Duong Vuong.

"Xich Quy, the Country of the Red Devils, was the name of Loc Tuc's territory. It was bounded on the north by Ho Nam Province, on the South by Chiem Thanh, on the West by Ba Thuc, and on the East by the South China Sea.

"Kinh Duong Vuong supposedly began his reign over Xich Quy in the year 2879 B.C., during which he one day called on the God of the Seas whose

daughter Long Nur he married. From this union
was born a son named Sung Lam. Sung Lam succeeded his father under the name of Lac Long
Quan."

Thus begins *A Short History of Viet-Nam*, by
Nguyen Van Thai and Nguyen Van Mung, published in Saigon in 1958. Fact and legend were in-
distinguishable, in those gentle, misty times of
unrecorded Vietnamese history. And as the authors
reflect in their writing, the ancient past still lies
heavy over the country. To the foreigner, there is
much in Vietnamese life that is whimsical, pic-
turesque, unchanging: the ancestral graves set in
paddy fields, the polite addressing of elders as
"Uncle," sturdy youths holding hands as they
stroll down a street, young women clad in colorful *ao dai* tunics and pantaloons and inevitably
riding bicycles, sidewalk vendors selling bronze
ornaments, black lacquer boxes, and shoes, wallets
and luggage made from elephant skins. The ancient crafts and customs are still very much a part
of Viet Nam today.

To be sure, other things are also a part of the
current Vietnamese scene. The terror of bombs
exploding on crowded streets killing men, women,
and children indiscriminately; civilian buses ambushed on rural roads; iron grates to protect patrons in Saigon restaurants and barbed wire and
earthworks to defend country villages; men beheaded, women tortured, and youths abducted.

Once again, Viet Nam is the Country of the Red Devils.

Yet, despite centuries-long periods of foreign domination, the Vietnamese have managed to maintain their national identity. Confucianism, brought and spread by Chinese conquerors, gave the Vietnamese moral unity and clear patterns of authority. Tightly-knit family clusters, the core of the hamlets and villages, provided continuity of culture and strong units of social tradition.

The legend continues that, during the golden era of the ruler Lac Long Quan, one of his hundred sons, Hung Vuong, founded the Hong Bang Dynasty which ruled until 258 B.C. It was succeeded by two later dynasties until, in 111 B.C., Nam Viet, as it was then known, was conquered by Chinese forces. Nam Viet became the Chinese province of Giao-Chi (meaning "Meeting Toes," because the people were pigeon-toed).

The first historical records concerning the Vietnamese in the Red River Delta were written by the Chinese before and after their conquest of the area. The Chinese found the Vietnamese organized in villages and groups of villages, led by hereditary chiefs who were in vassalage to provincial lords. These lords in turn owed allegiance to the king, to whom many of them were related. Agricultural methods were primitive. It was the Chinese who introduced the plow and the water buffalo.

The Chinese rule lasted more than one thousand years. There were occasional revolts, but none was successful. One of these rebellions was sparked by the repressive rule of a Chinese governor named To Dinh. The son-in-law of a local military chief was executed by To Dinh in 40 A.D. The widow, Trung Trac, and her sister, Trung Nhi, raised an army and succeeded in defeating the Chinese. The sisters proclaimed themselves queens and ruled for three years. But the Chinese sent powerful forces against them. The sisters were defeated and Chinese rule was restored. Trung Trac and Trung Nhi drowned themselves in the Hat River. The year was 43 A.D.

In Viet Nam, the memory of the warrior queens remains a symbol of resistance to foreign oppression. They are honored and worshiped at special pagodas, and annually young Vietnamese women, dressed entirely in white, parade in their honor.

This long history of Chinese domination is relevant to events in Viet Nam today, for, even while accepting some Chinese Communist assistance, the Communist North Vietnamese remain wary of falling under Chinese domination.

Independence was finally achieved when a Vietnamese general, Ngo Quyen, defeated the Chinese at the Battle of Bach Dang in 939. The Vietnamese named their new, independent state Dai Co Viet (Great Viet State). Despite a succession of Chinese invasions—including three by Kublai Khan in the thirteenth century—the Vietnamese managed to maintain their independence through a series of dynasties.

However, the final years of the Tran Dynasty (1225-1400) were a period of moral deterioration, with corruption and incompetence plaguing the administration. An ambitious regent named Le Qui Ly, claiming to be the descendant of a Chinese emperor, usurped the throne and changed his name to Ho Qui Ly. Using the restoration of the Tran Dynasty as a pretext, Chinese Emperor Thanh To invaded An Nam (the Chinese name for the land of the Vietnamese) and occupied it. By 1407 Dai Co Viet was once again a province of Imperial China.

The Chinese exploited the country and tried hard to Sinicize it. Forest products and precious metals were exported to China. Women were forced to wear Chinese fashions. Public instruction was in Chinese, and Chinese classics were substituted for the Vietnamese. Everyone was required to carry an identity card.

But these Chinese measures led only to the creation of a powerful resistance movement, with an aristocratic landowner, Le Loi, as its leader. In 1418 Le Loi began a guerrilla campaign which lasted a decade. In 1427, after a series of victories, the Vietnamese disarmed the Chinese and forced them back to their homeland. The Chinese occupation was ended.

In 1428 Le Loi came to the throne. He took the name Le Thai To and established a dynasty which was to rule until 1527. The Le rulers gave the government the general form it retained until the French conquered the land. The emperor was an absolute monarch as well as the religious head of the realm. The work of administering the country was in the hands of a civil bureaucracy selected by public examinations. At the village level, councils of elders had considerable freedom to manage local affairs, but were responsible for maintaining public order and for carrying out official decrees.

During the sixteenth and seventeenth centuries, Viet Nam was torn by regional strife as dynasties and powerful families fought for power and territory. Between 1545 and 1600 the country was partitioned between what was known as the "Northern Court" and the "Southern Court."

But of greater importance to history was the fact that the West reached Viet Nam in this era.

In 1535, a Portuguese captain, Antonio da Faria, arrived at Vung Da Nang. For the following century the Portuguese dominated trade with what they called Cochin-China. The Dutch, and then the English and French also began trade with the Vietnamese who were eager to obtain armaments for use in their internal conflicts.

With Western trade, Catholic missionaries arrived in Viet Nam. French missionaries played the prominent role, due to the fact that Portuguese power was declining, and the English and Dutch were interested chiefly in India and the Indies.

Confucian officials suspected the new religion, fearing it was the forerunner of conquest, and also believing that its morality based on the will of God conflicted with the Confucian concept of duty to family and state. Missionary activity was forbidden, but the ban was only sporadically enforced. Christianity spread among the poor, and Jesuit scholars trained in the sciences were welcomed at both the Northern and Southern Courts.

In 1771, three brothers of a Nguyen family in central Viet Nam led an uprising against the ruling Nguyen family, to whom they were probably not related. The campaign, lasting for more than fifteen years, was victorious for the brothers in both the North and the South, and by 1786 Viet Nam was reunited. In 1787 Nguyen Hue, one of the brothers, proclaimed himself Emperor Quang Trung. When Chinese Emperor Can Long launched a new invasion, Quang Trung ably defeated the Chinese forces.

The Quang Trung reign was to be brief, however, as Nguyen Anh, one of the deposed lords of the former ruling family in the South, invaded Viet Nam with his followers in 1787. After a struggle that lasted until 1802, Nguyen Anh proclaimed himself Emperor Gia Long and changed the name

of the country from An Nam to Viet Nam. This
Nguyen Dynasty survived until the abdication
of Emperor Bao Dai in 1945.

The late eighteenth century saw the beginnings
of significant French involvement in Vietnamese
affairs. At one time, the life of Nguyen Anh, who
became Emperor Gia Long, had been saved by a
French missionary, Monseigneur Pigneau de
Behaine, Bishop of Adran. The Emperor later
sought the assistance of the Bishop, who hoped
to place a Christian on the Vietnamese throne.
The Bishop arranged an alliance in which France
promised military assistance in return for com-
mercial concessions, as well as the port of Tourane
(now Da Nang) and the island of Poulo Condore
(now Con Son). Disagreements in France, however, blocked aid for the Emperor, and the Bishop
privately raised a small force of Frenchmen. The
Bishop liked to accompany Gia Long to the bat-
tlefields, and it was on such an occasion in 1799
that he died.

Gia Long did not accept the Christian faith as
the Bishop had hoped, but out of gratitude to
him, he did not persecute Christians. His suc-
cessors, however, were not so tolerant and repressed
both missionaries and the sizable communities of
converts that existed. This persecution was a factor
in drawing increasing French attention to Viet
Nam. In addition, there were mounting pressures
inside France aimed at establishing a French posi-

tion in Viet Nam, much as other European powers were establishing themselves elsewhere in Asia. A conquest, the French felt, would boost national prestige and provide both military advantages and trade benefits.

A French attack on Tourane was made in 1847 and Vietnamese ships were sunk in the port. Another attack was launched in 1856, when a French admiral arrived at Tourane and protested the Vietnamese persecution of Catholics. Receiving no reply, the French fired on Vietnamese military posts and then departed.

In 1858, an expeditionary force of 15 warships and 1500 French troops, plus 850 Filipino troops supplied by France's ally Spain, attacked and captured Tourane. The French conquest of Viet Nam had begun. In 1861, Saigon fell, and in the following years the French annexed first the southern portions of Viet Nam and then the northern sections. Chinese troops were sent to assist the Vietnamese, but these combined forces were unable to prevent the French conquest. Under the Treaty of Qui Mui, signed August 23, 1883, the Vietnamese accepted a French protectorate over their land, and under the Fournier Agreement, signed the following year, China recognized the protectorate. Despite the accords, there would still be more battles, but the French were never seriously threatened.

French colonial rule then became firmly en-

trenched. In the three sections of what is now Viet
Nam, the degree of French control varied only
slightly in each. In An Nam (central Viet Nam),
the emperor and his officials retained authority
over internal affairs, except for customs fees and
public works, but the French watched carefully
and kept the right to maintain troops in the area.
In Tonkin (northern Viet Nam) and Cochin-China
(southern Vietnam) there were even fewer concessions to local autonomy. The French controlled
administration, and only subordinate positions
were open to Vietnamese.

French rule was extended to Cambodia in 1867,
when Siam (Thailand), which had long dominated
Cambodia, recognized a French protectorate over
that land, in return for Siamese annexation of two
Cambodian provinces. Then, in 1893, following a
display of French naval strength off Bangkok,
Siam, France also annexed Laos. All of the French-
occupied territories were organized as the Indochinese Federation under a French governor-
general.

While Indochina was a colony to be exploited,
still, French rule did benefit the area, too. The
French opened schools and hospitals, established
various public services, and inaugurated the Indochinese University in 1906. This was followed by
other centers of higher learning, including schools
of veterinary medicine, pedagogy, agriculture,
commerce, fine arts, and applied sciences. The

French developed rice lands in the fertile Mekong Delta and rubber plantations in the central highlands. Mines were dug, industries developed, and transportation networks established.

French rule, however, was not unchallenged. There were uprisings, secret societies, intellectual ferment, deepening nationalism. Japan's victory over Russia in 1905 gave impetus to Asian nationalists who saw that a Western power could be defeated by Asians. There were the inevitable resentments of a people ruled by foreigners.

Despite the unrest, France managed to maintain firm control over Indochina until World War II. When the Japanese entered the war and began their military drive southward, the pro-Axis French regime at Vichy was in nominal power in unoccupied France and it still controlled Indochina. The French and Japanese were, therefore, at least theoretical allies. On July 29, 1941, an agreement was signed which defined the relations between the French and Japanese in Indochina for "the common defense of Indochina." The Japanese were permitted to use eight airports and the naval bases at Saigon and Cam Ranh. The French colonial administrative structure remained intact, and French troops continued their garrison duties. Japan, however, under an economic agreement, was to receive all of Indochina's major exports, including rice, manganese, tungsten, antimony, tin, and chrome.

While this *modus vivendi* continued between the French and Japanese, an entirely different venture was beginning in the interior. On May 19, 1941, under the leadership of a Communist revolutionary, Ho Chi Minh, the *Viet Nam Doc Lap Dong Minh Hoi* (League for the Independence of Viet Nam) had been established. For thirty years, Communist organization in Southeast Asia had consisted of a variety of activities, and the group which surrounded Ho Chi Minh had been at the center of that organization. They maintained a considerable identity within the world-wide Communist system. The name *Viet Nam Doc Lap Dong Minh Hoi*—better known as the Viet Minh—was chosen by the Indochinese Communist Party as a popular-front name which would muster support from the populace that the Party could not. During the war years, the Viet Minh grew slowly in strength, setting up jungle bases, organizing and training guerrilla forces, and extending its control through rural areas where neither the French nor Japanese ventured.

By 1945 it was apparent that the Axis was losing the war. Paris had been liberated, the Vichy government had fallen. The French in Indochina became increasingly reluctant to cooperate with the Japanese. On March 9, 1945, at eight o'clock in the evening, the Japanese Ambassador handed the French Governor-General an ultimatum demanding that all French forces be put under the supreme command of the Japanese. That night the Japanese Army struck, seizing power throughout Indochina and interning French military and civilian officials as well as French soldiers. Viet Nam was proclaimed to be "independent," and a puppet regime was established under Emperor Bao Dai.

With the defeat of the Japanese forces in the Pacific later that year, Japanese control in Indochina collapsed. The puppet regime also fell apart, and Bao Dai abdicated, handing over his imperial seal and other symbols of office to Ho Chi Minh, who had earlier announced the formation of a "Committee for the Liberation of the Vietnamese People" with himself as president. The Communist-dominated Viet Minh, which at that time also included non-Communist nationalist elements, was in virtual control of the country. On September 2, 1945, Ho Chi Minh announced the formation of a provisional government and the establishment of the "Democratic Republic of Viet Nam." This is the moment at which the stage was set for terror.

Under Communist-trained Ho, it was inevitable that what started theoretically as an anti-colonial "liberation," would not stop until Ho Chi Minh's terror tactics had been used against his fellow countrymen in an attempt to bring the entire country under Communist rule.

World War II had created revolutionary conditions in many countries throughout the world.

Circumstances in Indochina, however, were particularly favorable for Communist insurgents. As described by George Modelski in his essay on the Viet Minh, the crumbling of colonial rule had been accelerated to a great degree by the stationing of Japanese troops in Indochina from 1940 onward.* On the other hand, the ending of colonial rule had not been balanced by the appearance of strong nationalist groups. The Japanese had flirted with certain Vietnamese nationalists from 1940 to 1945, but the Japanese overthrow of French power came too late for the cabinet of the Emperor Bao Dai to establish itself firmly in the country before the Japanese capitulation in the Pacific. What resulted, therefore, was pure turmoil.

Into this vacuum of authority—a basic condition for insurrectionary success, as Modelski points out—stepped the Viet Minh, ably led from the background by the Communist Party of Indochina.

Modelski writes that when Ho Chi Minh returned to the Sino-Vietnamese border region, after an extensive visit to the USSR and China from 1932 to 1941, he called a session of the Communist Party's Central Committee in May of that year. It was on the following day that the Viet Minh

* George Modelski, "Viet Minh," in *Communism and Revolution,* edited by C. E. Black and T. P. Thornton (Princeton, N. J.: Princeton University Press, 1964).

Front was officially founded. The men who assumed direction of the party, with Ho Chi Minh,
on that day in 1941 have remained leaders of the
Viet Minh complex to this day.

The official history of the Viet Minh, according
to Modelski, summarizes the fundamentals of
guerrilla warfare: "reliance on the masses, con-
tinual growth, extreme mobility and constant
adaptation." These fundamentals were thoroughly
learned, and the basis for the seizure of power
was established in those crucial years from 1941
through 1945.

Within the councils of the victorious Allied nations there was disagreement over the future of
Indochina. France, supported by Great Britain,
wanted Indochina returned to its control. Nationalist China opposed this. And the United States
advocated establishment of an international trus-
teeship. The French-British view prevailed, and it
was agreed that Indochina should be returned to
France. As a preliminary step, the British were to
accept the surrender of the Japanese south of the
16th parallel, and Chinese forces would accept the
surrender north of that line.

British troops arrived in Saigon on September
12, 1945. On September 22, they released im-
prisoned French paratroopers and armed them.
That night the paratroopers seized City Hall and
other key places in Saigon. The French spread out

from Saigon and within months had regained
control of South Viet Nam. On January 28, the
British withdrew from Viet Nam.

The occupation of the northern portion of the
country by the French was more difficult because
of the reluctance of the Chinese to leave. When
French warships and troop ships approached the
port of Haiphong, they were met by Chinese artillery fire, and the French did not land. But the
Chinese did eventually withdraw from Indochina,
under an agreement in which they recognized the
French return, and the French relinquished all of
their extraterritorial rights in China.

The Viet Minh favored the French over the
Chinese, figuring that it would be easier to dislodge the French than the Chinese, age-old enemies of the Vietnamese. The French and the Viet
Minh ("Government of the Republic of Viet
Nam") signed an agreement on March 6, 1946,
under which France recognized Viet Nam as "an
independent state . . . and a part of the Indochinese Federation within the French Union." In
return, the Viet Minh agreed to "welcome the
French troops in accordance with international
treaties when they come to take over from the
Chinese troops."

The accord, however, was at best superficial and
temporary. Fundamentally, the French wanted to
retain control over Indochina, and the Communists and nationalists wanted an independent state.

There were additional negotiations, but trouble was inevitable, and trouble was not long in coming. Street battles and skirmishes led to open hostilities. In November, 1946, shooting broke out in Haiphong, and the subsequent French bombardment of the city reportedly killed more than 6000 Vietnamese. On the night of December 19, 1946, the Viet Minh attacked the French in Hanoi, Hue, and other cities, and a full-scale war was under way.

It was a war that would last eight years and cost the French 35,000 killed and 48,000 wounded. Financially, it was disastrous. The United States gave France and Viet Nam aid totaling more than $4,000,000,000. Communist China and other Communist nations expended large sums in aiding the Viet Minh.

In the early months of 1947, the French forces established control over the principal towns in central and north Viet Nam, where the Viet Minh were strongest. This forced the Viet Minh to adopt the guerrilla tactics which became the chief characteristic of the conflict. Ho Chi Minh's guerrillas shrewdly used the jungle to neutralize French power and mobility. Selecting their targets, striking at opportune moments, withdrawing when faced with superior strength, the Communists fought a war that found the French on the defensive as often as the offensive.

It was clear that as long as the French relied on

military warfare alone and did not provide the
Vietnamese nationals with a political rallying
point, there was little hope of victory. The French,
therefore, sought out the Emperor Bao Dai. A
number of Vietnamese nationalists and anti-Com-
munist political groups were prepared to support
Bao Dai against Ho Chi Minh, and a National
Union Front formed around the emperor. Eventually, after prolonged negotiations, an agreement
was signed with Bao Dai on June 5, 1948, recog-
nizing the independence of the Associated State of
Viet Nam within the French Union.

But the anti-Communists were slow to unite,
primarily because of French reluctance to deliver
real sovereignty to the new state. Nevertheless, in
1949, the French agreed to a Vietnamese army
for internal security purposes and an Indochina
bank for Vietnam as well as a number of con-
ferences on foreign trade, customs, and immigration. In 1951, an agreement gave the Viet Nam
government the administration of immigration,
communications, foreign trade, customs, and finances, albeit with French rights reserved. These
sovereign rights, slowly acquired and exercised,
were to prepare the Associated State for the as-
sumption of full power when complete independence eventually came.

Meawhile, as the French were slow to relinquish
political power to the Vietnamese, so the military
struggle became essentially one between the French

and the Viet Minh. After three years of struggle, in 1950 the Viet Minh gained control of large areas of the countryside. The French firmly held the large cities. Chinese Communist aid led to major Viet Minh victories that gave them control of the Chinese border provinces and a great part of North Viet Nam (Tonkin). But when the Viet Minh attempted a major offensive in the Red River Delta designed to take Hanoi, they were severely defeated in a battle with French troops and by the forerunners of the Vietnamese army.

In December of 1950, the French dispatched to Viet Nam one of their foremost military leaders, General de Lattre de Tassigny. The already-famous general developed a plan to build a strong line of bunkers in the Red River Delta and to regroup French forces therein. He also made a strong call for the build up of Vietnamese forces to defend their own country, and by 1953 there actually was a Vietnamese army of some 150,000 men. De Lattre de Tassigny's bunker strategy was not successful. The guerrillas took advantage of the exposed disposition of French troops to strike direct blows from the rear. Whether or not the general might eventually have been successful cannot be known, for he returned home in December, 1951, and was dead of cancer early in 1952.

The French command in Indochina was then assumed by General Henri Navarre. He envisaged the organization of a strong strategic mobile force which would be capable of breaking up the Communist offensives and annihilating the main part of their forces. Navarre ordered withdrawal from certain posts and the regroupment of his picked European and African units into mobile forces. New units from France, West Germany, North Africa, and Korea were rushed to the Indochina front. By the autumn of 1953, French mobile forces totaled 84 battalions.

The Navarre plan presented a serious threat to the Viet Minh. Now that the French were concentrating their forces in the Red River Delta and keeping the Viet Minh off balance with swift powerful strikes into their zone, the Viet Minh had to decide whether to face the French in strength, persist in the prolonged guerrilla campaign, or use their forces for attacks in other directions. The Viet Minh decided upon a policy of taking the initiative and maintaining their mobility, striking toward the Laotian border and moving into Laos to assist the Communist forces there. The French had wanted to retain the initiative by concentrating the fighting in the Red River Delta. Now they were obliged to disperse their forces to protect themselves on the Laotian border as well. The war appeared once more stalemated.

On the political front, however, the various forces were moving toward a settlement. In 1953, the French took some steps toward establishment of the complete independence of Viet Nam within the French Union, hoping to diffuse thereby the Viet Minh claims of representing the Vietnamese people. This program was still under negotiation when the world powers agreed to a peace conference of all parties.

In April, 1954, a conference was convened in Geneva to seek an end to the Indochina conflict. Present at the Geneva Conference were representatives of France, the Democratic Republic of Viet Nam (Viet Minh), the Associated States of Viet Nam, Cambodia, and Laos, Communist China, Great Britain, the United States, and North and South Korea.

Even as the meeting convened, one last great battle was in progress at the heavily fortified town of Dien Bien Phu. After 55 days and 55 nights of fighting, the French garrison was all but annihilated. On May 7, 1954, one of the most gallant defenses of modern times ended.

On July 21, the conferees agreed to the complete independence of Cambodia, Laos, and Viet Nam. It was decided, in the case of Viet Nam, to partition the country along the 17th parallel. The French and South Vietnamese would remove all of their forces from north of that line; the Viet Minh would evacuate all their troops from south of the parallel. The Viet Minh Government was given *de facto* recognition of its sovereignty in the North. This was known as the 1954 Geneva Agreement. Neither the South Vietnamese nor the

United States Government accepted the terms, but simply "noted" them.

The French had lost a battle, not the war, at Dien Bien Phu. They still held strong positions and substantial military forces remained. In the view of Hoang Van-Chi, an official of the Viet Minh at the time of the Geneva Conference who later defected, the French had been hasty in signing the agreement. "If the French were war-weary, the DRV [Viet Minh] was close to bankruptcy, at least so far as material resources were concerned."*

But a war-weary public opinion in France did push the political leaders to the conference table agreement. The prewar system of colonies was, in any event, a dying cause, unpopular world-wide; there were problems in other overseas territories in Africa; and, at home, France had made only the beginnings of domestic recovery from World War II when the Vietnamese fighting started draining its strength. The French would now withdraw entirely from Indochina.

Viet Nam at last knew an uneasy peace. But it was not to continue for long. The ancient land of Xich Quy still had its Red Devils.

---

* Hoang Van-Chi, *From Colonialism to Communism* (New York: Frederick A. Praeger, 1964).

Chapter II

THE TERROR MAKERS

"Peace does not mean everlasting peace." These were the words of Ho Chi Minh himself in July of 1954, even before the ink had dried on the agreements reached at Geneva. The Communists had never relinquished their goal of conquering all of Viet Nam—the foundations for which were laid between 1941 and 1945—and the start of terrorist activities in South Viet Nam in 1957 signaled the beginning of a new Communist campaign of conquest.

Even before this, however, the Communists were making preparations for future war and subversion. When Viet Nam was partitioned, thousands of carefully selected Party members were ordered to remain in the South and to keep their clandestine apparatus intact. Arms and ammunition were stored for future use. Some guerrilla fighters rejoined their families to await the Party's call, and others withdrew to remote jungle and mountain hideouts. Some 90,000 moved to North Viet Nam and, after receiving thorough training in terror techniques, they would later infiltrate back into South Viet Nam.

Viet Nam was to become a classic instance of the use of the tactic of terror. The Communists have waged war, and the Communists have also waged violence. War is, of course, violence, but violence is not always war. War is formal conflict between forces of armed men. Violence is manifest in terror, in this case inflicted by armed men on helpless civilians. This is the violence that the Communists have been waging against the people of South Viet Nam.

In an article published in July, 1964, General Vo Nguyen Giap, commander of North Vietnamese military forces, wrote:

"... *The most correct path to be followed by the peoples to liberate themselves is revolutionary violence and revolutionary war.* [The italics are Giap's.] This path conforms strictly to the ethics and the fundamentals of Marxism-Leninism on class struggle, on the state and the revolution. . . .

"Revolutionary violence takes up many forms: political violence, armed violence, and armed violence combined with political violence. Basing ourselves on our absolute superiority in the political field, and on the policy of the enemy who uses military as well as political means to quell the revolution, our southern compatriots are now using political violence combined with armed violence against the enemy. They have known how to take advantage of and to develop the valuable experiences gained by all our people in the revolutionary struggles they have waged up to the present time."

Communist dialecticians are masters of euphemism. For *"armed violence,"* read "guerrilla warfare." For *"political violence,"* read, "violence with a political purpose"; i.e., the murder of a village chief in order to eliminate a political enemy.

The story of Vietnamese Communism began in 1890 in Kim Lien Village in Nghe An Province. There, a son, Nguyen Tat Thanh, was born to a local scholar. Nguyen would bear many names in the years to come, but the one by which history has come to know him is Ho Chi Minh.

Ho was educated in Saigon and the city of Hue. Later he became a teacher. In 1912 he traveled to Europe as a cook's helper aboard a merchant ship. In the period that followed he did considerably more traveling, including trips to Africa and the United States. He held a variety of jobs, working as a servant to a French family in Le Havre and as a boilerman at the Carlton Hotel in London. At the Versailles Peace Conference in 1919, he submitted a "List of Claims of the Vietnamese People," demanding greater rights for the Vietnamese. The Conference ignored Ho.

But Ho would be heard from. He had become

a disciple of Karl Marx. He wrote pamphlets, edited an anti-colonial weekly, *Le Paria* ("The Outcast"), and went to Moscow in June, 1923, to attend the International Peasants' Conference. He was elected to the Executive Committee of this organization. The following year he attended the Fifth Congress of the Communist International, also held in Moscow. He addressed the delegates, telling them of starvation and poverty in all French colonies and calling on the Communist International to "help them organize themselves and supply them with leading cadres and guide them to the revolution and liberation."

In the years that followed, Ho traveled a number of times to Russia and China, did organizational work, made another trip to Europe, wrote a book called *The Revolutionary Path,* and trained Communist cadres to infiltrate French Indochina.

Three separate Communist parties had been established in Indochina. The Communist International declared that this division constituted "a very great danger for the future of the Indochinese revolution," and it ordered that a "united party" be created. Ho went to Hong Kong to convene a conference of unification, of which he was chairman, and on February 3, 1930, the Vietnamese Communist Party was officially organized.

In 1940, after an absence of twenty-eight years, Ho returned to Indochina. Operating from the mountain caves of Cao Bang Province, he published a newspaper, trained Communist cadres, and pressed forward with organizational work that culminated in the establishment on May 19, 1941, of the Viet Minh.

During the years of Japanese occupation of Indochina, Ho deftly maintained relations with the Chinese Communists, with Chiang Kai-shek's Nationalists, and with American officials. He received assistance from all three quarters, and thus he was able to build up a signficant guerrilla force, commanded by a tough teacher-turned-soldier named Vo Nguyen Giap. Japanese authority was almost entirely confined to urban areas, and the Viet Minh were able to take over the countryside. The Communists were less concerned with harassing the Japanese than with entrenching themselves.

Upon the capitulation of Japan and the march of the Chinese Army into Indochina, some Communist factions advocated a campaign against the Chinese, historic foes of the Vietnamese, but Ho preferred to play the French against the Chinese, reportedly declaring, "I prefer to smell French *merde* for five years than smell the Chinese variety for the rest of my life." Ho believed that the French would be an easier foe for the Vietnamese to dislodge from Indochina than the Chinese—if the French would first get the Chinese out.

The Chinese did get out and the French did

return. Giap, in his book, *People's War, People's Army,* has given the Communist view of events in those days:

". . . In Hanoi, the capital, on September 2nd [1945], the provisional government was formed around President Ho Chi Minh; it presented itself to the nation, proclaimed the independence of Viet Nam, and called on the nation to unite, to hold itself in readiness to defend the country and to oppose all attempts at imperialist aggression. The Democratic Republic of Viet Nam was born, the first people's democracy in Southeast Asia.

"But the imperialists intended to nip the republican regime in the bud and once again transform Viet Nam into a colony. Three weeks had hardly gone by when, on September 23rd, 1945, the French Expeditionary Corps opened fire in Saigon. The whole Vietnamese nation then rose to resist foreign aggression. From that day, began a war of national liberation which was to be carried on for nine years. . . ."

During those nine years, the French poured men, materiel, and their best military brainpower into the struggle. They could not crush the Viet Minh, however, and, finally, with the Geneva Conference in 1954, the war came to an end.

The Conference set up an independent North Viet Nam, under President Ho Chi Minh. It also established South Viet Nam, where nationalism was equally strong, but the Viet Minh was not.

To South Viet Nam fled a million refugees from the North who did not agree with Ho. When peace was restored and conditions suitable for democratic elections existed, elections were to be held on the question of a united Viet Nam.

But conditions suitable for elections never came about. During the late 1950's the terror campaign and guerrilla operations were steadily expanded in South Viet Nam, covertly assisted by Ho's government in Hanoi. In time, this assistance became less covert. Pressure from the North increased until it took on the proportions of actual internal war. The first step took the form of the elimination of "traitors" (officials, village chiefs, teachers).

The signal for full-scale war was given at the Third Congress of the *Lao Dong* (Workers') Party (i.e., the Communist Party), held in Hanoi in September, 1960. The Congress set two tasks for its members: "to carry out the socialist revolution in North Viet Nam" and "to liberate South Viet Nam from the ruling yoke of the U.S. imperialists and their henchmen in order to achieve national unity and complete independence and freedom throughout the country." Addressing the Congress, Ho spoke of the necessity "to step up the socialist revolution in the North and, at the same time, to step up the national democratic people's revolution in the South."

The *Lao Dong* Congress called on Communists in the South "to rally all national and democratic

forces, [and to] expand and consolidate the national unity bloc." Once again the tactic of a
"Popular Front" including alleged non-Communists was adopted. On December 20, 1960, the
National Front for Liberation of South Viet Nam
(the Viet Cong) was formally established. Radio
Hanoi declared that the Front's "sacred historical
task" was "to liberate the South." In the Communist view, North Viet Nam was the springboard
for the assault on the South. Call it "national reunification," "democratic revolution," "liberation"
or whatever, it still remained Communist double
talk for subversion.

George Modelski, in the article already men-
tioned, states that by September, 1961, the Front
for the Liberation of the South, a replica of the
earlier Viet Minh National Front, claimed control
of more than 90 per cent of the six thousand villages of South Viet Nam. Prompt and determined
American assistance to South Viet Nam and the
psychological effect of the settlement reached between the United States and Laos altered Viet
Minh policy somewhat. The high-sounding objective of national reunification was relegated to
the background, and work on the revolution by
direct armed struggle remained in the preparatory
stage. However, terror and guerrilla tactics were
being increasingly used.

Modelski notes that the models used by the
Viet Minh have been varied. The distance from

Moscow, and the circumstances of war which made necessary a clandestine existence for the leadership, dictated the pursuit of policies attuned to local conditions and of great flexibility. This freedom did not weaken the Viet Minh ties of allegiance to the International movement of the Soviet Party, for the Vietnamese Communist Party continues to be the brains and organization center of the entire Viet Minh complex.

The Viet Minh have been engaged on one front or another for twenty years. Their jungle warfare tactics are nearly perfect, more skillful than those of guerrillas, according to Modelski. They are the tactics of a fully trained and well-equipped army, with a flexibility of operation gained from a fine intelligence system based on broad and effective political networks. The application of violence in Viet Minh tactics, Modelski continues, extends beyond military targets. It includes calculated elimination of anyone who might potentially support or form the core of opposition to its policies. In fact, according to his information, by 1957-1958, the deliberate policy of exterminating possible opponents had been refined to an art, with South Vietnamese village chiefs serving as primary targets for wholesale campaigns of assassination.

Although a certain amount of terrorism is not unexpected in revolutionary wars, Modelski notes that one cannot help thinking that, "In Viet Minh tactics this has long passed the stage of excess and has become a vice, an intoxication with violence, one that may well be a release from the terrible and inhumanly prolonged hardships and repressions of personal interests which its adherents must undergo."

A North Vietnamese booklet portrays the National Front for South Viet Nam (Viet Cong) as aiming at uniting all sections of the population, setting up a unified national democratic government to achieve independence, peace, neutrality, freedom, and democracy in an advance toward national reunification. The organization of the National Liberation Front (N.L.F.) was as follows:

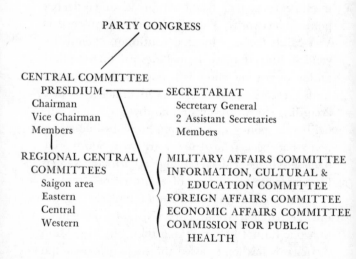

PARTY CONGRESS

CENTRAL COMMITTEE
   PRESIDIUM —————— SECRETARIAT
   Chairman   Secretary General
   Vice Chairman   2 Assistant Secretaries
   Members   Members

REGIONAL CENTRAL   MILITARY AFFAIRS COMMITTEE
   COMMITTEES   INFORMATION, CULTURAL &
   Saigon area   EDUCATION COMMITTEE
   Eastern   FOREIGN AFFAIRS COMMITTEE
   Central   ECONOMIC AFFAIRS COMMITTEE
   Western   COMMISSION FOR PUBLIC
                     HEALTH

While retaining complete control of the Front, the Communists wanted to give it the appearance of a broad representation. They sought well-known non-Communists from South Viet Nam who would give it prestige. But they failed in their efforts to obtain suitable personnel. Although the first Central Committee, announced in March of 1962, reserved places for 52 members, it actually contained only 31 members—most of whom were hitherto unknown. Communist propaganda claimed that the meeting at which the Committee was elected was heavily attended and "truly representative of the people." In fact, fewer than two hundred persons participated.

The second Central Committee, announced in January of 1964, had 41 members. Of the 31 members of the first Committee, only about half stayed on to the second, indicating that the rest had proved unsuitable for their posts. Most of the top leaders had long been associated with the Communists. The Chairman of the Central Committee, Nguyen Huu Tho, is a lawyer who has participated in Communist activities in Viet Nam since 1947. The Secretary General of the Front, Huynh Tan Phat, led a minor political party into the Viet Minh in the early 1950's and has been a Communist follower ever since. Tran Buu Khiem, head of the Foreign Affairs Committee, is believed to have been one of the organizers of the Viet Cong military effort and a former chief of security for the Communist organization in South Viet Nam.

Behind the publicly acknowledged leaders of the National Liberation Front there is another, clandestine group of hard-core Communist leaders. Most of them belong to the North Vietnamese *Lao Dong* Party, and also to the South Vietnamese People's Revolutionary Party (P.R.P.). The P.R.P. was evidently organized late in 1961, and its founding was announced the following January. The Communists sought to make it appear that the P.R.P. was a local South Vietnamese party, organized by the South Vietnamese Communists.

Actually, the P.R.P. is nothing more than the South Vietnamese branch of the *Lao Dong* Party. This was revealed in a *Lao Dong* Central Committee resolution which was secretly adopted in November of 1961: "First of all, it must be clearly understood that this is only a name change. Although the overt name is different from what it is in North Viet Nam, nevertheless, secretly . . . the Party segment in South Viet Nam is a segment of the *Lao Dong* Party under the leadership of the Party Central Committee, headed by Chairman Ho. . . . Except for the name, there is no change whatever."

The hard-core leaders of the P.R.P. are shadowy figures. Muoi Cuc, a Communist for more than twenty years and one-time Viet Minh political commissar for the Saigon area during the war against the French, is believed to be the top Communist military-political leader in South Viet Nam. He is said to run the overall Communist headquarters, the so-called Central Office for South Viet Nam. One of the top military chiefs under Cuc is Major General Nguyen Don, former commander of the North Vietnamese 305th Division. Another military leader is Major General Hoang Khiet, who has appeared in North Viet Nam to address soldiers being trained for infiltration into the South.

In addition to controlling politically the subversive campaign in South Viet Nam, North Viet Nam has also provided a major quantity of material and manpower support. Special training camps operated by the North Vietnamese Army give political and military training to men who are to infiltrate into South Viet Nam. At first, a good many of the infiltrators were former South Vietnamese, but later, increasing numbers of North Vietnamese were sent south—sometimes entire combat units of the North Vietnamese Army.

The infiltration process began in the late 1950's, when the Communists opened their drive to conquer South Viet Nam. In 1959 and 1960, at least 1800 men moved into South Viet Nam from the North. The flow increased to more than 3700 in 1961 and to at least 5400 in 1962. During 1965, North Viet Nam stepped up its infiltration program considerably, and by November of that year

at least seven full regiments of the North Vietnamese Army were engaged in the war below the
border.

The North Vietnamese selected to be trained
to infiltrate into the South remain under the discipline of the Military High Command in Hanoi.
Their principal training center is at Xuan Mai
near Hanoi. There is another center at Thanh
Hoa. Upon completion of their courses—military,
political, and propaganda subjects—the infiltrators are usually moved to Vinh on the coast. Some
go to a staging area at Dong Hoi, where they receive final training.

Then the men are taken by truck to the Laotian
border. Their transportation through Laos is arranged by the 70th Transportation Group of the
North Vietnamese Army. At the Laotian border
the infiltrators turn in their North Vietnamese uniforms and all personal papers, notebooks, and
photographs. Some have been outfitted with Laotian uniforms for their passage through that country. They usually move along the Laos–South Viet
Nam border and then turn eastward, entering
South Viet Nam in Quang Nam, Quang Tri, or
one of the other border provinces.

The Communists have established regular lanes
into the South, with way stations about one day's
march apart. The stations are equipped to feed
and quarter the infiltrators and provide medical
treatment where required. Local guides lead the

men along the trails, from halfway between two stations, through their own base station, and halfway to the next base. Thus, the guides know only their own immediate sectors. As a further security precaution, only leaders of the infiltrating groups are permitted to talk with the guides.

The newly-arriving terrorists carry a three-to-five-days supply of food, plus a packet of medicines and bandages. They have usually been issued two unmarked uniforms, a sweater, rubber sandals, a hammock, mosquito netting, waterproof sheeting, and black civilian pajama-like suits. (The black pajamas are not uniforms of the Viet Cong, but the standard clothing of the rural Vietnamese among whom the Viet Cong hide.)

The size of infiltration groups vary. They may be as small as five men, or as large as five hundred; a rough average is forty to fifty men. Within South Viet Nam, the groups are handled by Viet Cong transportation units. They may remain intact as a combat unit within the Viet Cong forces, or they may be split up and assigned to various Viet Cong units.

Following are three examples of typical infiltrators. Their very typicality is one of the great dangers. Any one of these men could be among the countless thousands of unknown faces met on the crowded city streets, or he could be the lone, black-clad peasant, returning from his rice paddy in the evening.

Tran Ngoc Linh is the son of a middle-class farm family who served with the Viet Minh against the French and then moved to North Viet Nam in 1954. He spent the next seven years in the North Vietnamese Army. In September of 1962, Linh was assigned to the Xuan Mai training center to prepare for duty in South Viet Nam. His group was given a four-month refresher course in infantry tactics, with emphasis on guerrilla fighting, and then he received six months of training in the use of machine guns against aircraft.

Linh and about 120 others were assigned to the 406th Infiltration Group, commanded by a senior captain. They were divided into four platoons. During the final weeks of training they were issued new equipment, including black pajamas, a khaki uniform, a hammock, mosquito netting, and other supplies.

In the early morning hours of July 4, 1963, the group started the journey from Xuan Mai. A convoy of six trucks moved south along Highway 21, and on July 7 arrived at the final processing station near the Laos—North Viet Nam border. Here, the men turned in their North Vietnamese uniforms and their personal papers.

There were delays, and not until August did the group set out through Laos. Twice along the way Linh was delayed, due to illness, and was left behind by the group. Finally, during the first week of November, Linh began the final leg of a journey to a Viet Cong center, where he would be assigned to a combat unit. He and three others, who had also been delayed because of malaria and other ills, comprised a group. Moving through the jungles of Quang Duc Province near the Cambodian border, they met a South Vietnamese Army unit on the morning of November 9. One of the infiltrators was killed, two escaped, and Linh was captured.

Dao Kien Lap, a civilian radio technician, had been a member of the Communist Party in North Viet Nam since 1955. In February of 1963, he was selected for infiltration into South Viet Nam. Lap was part of a group of about 70 civilian specialists, including doctors, pharmacists, radio technicians, union organizers, youth organizers, propagandists, a newspaper publisher, and a member of the Hanoi city government.

The group received three months of basic military training and then departed for the South in mid-June. Their orders were to report to the Viet Cong Central Office in South Viet Nam, where they would be given assignments in accordance with their specialties. Lap and the publisher were to help operate a radio station.

They traveled through Laos and entered South Viet Nam. In Quang Nam Province they rested for several weeks to recuperate from their arduous travels. On October 1, they were led by guides to a Viet Cong station in Ban Me Thuot.

By then, however, Lap had decided to defect. He set out with one companion, from whom he became separated, and surrendered at a government post on October 13.

Vo Thoi was born in Quang Ngai Province in South Viet Nam in 1932. He served with the Viet Minh fighting against the French. When the fighting ended, he was transferred to North Viet Nam with his unit. He remained in the North Vietnamese Army until 1960, at which time he was sent to work on a state farm.

In September of 1962, Vo was told he must join the newly activated 22nd Battalion, all of whose members had originally come from South Viet Nam. The battalion was given a six-month training course, which included political indoctrination, squad to company combat tactics, and guerrilla and counterguerrilla techniques.

On March 5, 1963, the 22nd Battalion was ordered to move south. It was transported in trucks to Dong Hoi, just north of the 17th parallel, and from there it moved westward and across the Laotian border. The unit of more than three hundred men marched by day and rested by night, following mountain trails in the border area. Every fifth day there was a full day's rest at a way station. One company turned off the trail at Thua Thien Province, but Vo and the remainder continued. Two additional companies from a neighboring province joined the battalion in Binh Dinh

Province. The battalion's assignment was to harass hamlets, seize rice and cattle, kill or kidnap Government officials, and recruit local youth for the Viet Cong.

On the night of October 7, 1963, Vo's unit attacked An Tuong village and succeeded in overrunning it. Vo's company—Vo held the rank of sergeant—then set up an ambush to trap South Vietnamese troops rushing to aid the village. In the ensuing fight Vo was seriously wounded. He was taken prisoner by local farmers and turned over to the South Vietnamese authorities.

When the Communists began their campaign of subversion and terrorism against South Viet Nam, they relied mainly on stocks of weapons and ammunition left behind from the war against the French. The supplies sent in from North Viet Nam were also largely of the same origin. Later, as the military campaign progressed, the Viet Cong were able to arm themselves with weapons captured from Government forces.

But as the conflict has expanded in scope—particularly with the participation of well-equipped American forces—the Viet Cong have had a growing need for a greater number of modern weapons. North Viet Nam has had to provide increasing quantities of military supplies.

More and more weapons of Communist origin have been captured in South Viet Nam, including

Russian M-33 grenades, North Vietnamese 81mm. mortars, and Chinese Communist 7.92mm. heavy machine guns. Chinese Communist weapons have been particularly numerous and have also included 7.62mm. semi-automatic carbines, 7.62mm. light machine guns, 7.62mm. assault rifles, 75mm. recoilless rifles, mortars and mortar shells, grenades, submachine guns, blocks of TNT, and anti-tank grenade launchers and ammunition. One Viet Cong prisoner told his captors that his entire company had been supplied with modern Chinese weapons.

Materiel is sent into South Viet Nam from the North by a variety of methods—overland, by river and canal, and by sea. A few sampans can transport a considerable quantity of weapons—much more readily than porters carrying it through jungles and over mountain trails. South Viet Nam has thousands of miles of coastline, rivers, and canals, and the use of boats is therefore a preferred means for the transport of materials by the Viet Cong.

On February 18, 1965, an American helicopter pilot flying along the South Vietnamese coast sighted a suspicious vessel. It was a small cargo ship, carefully camouflaged and moored just offshore on the coast of Phu Yen Province.

Fighter planes were summoned and, as they approached the vessel, they met machine gun fire from the deck of the ship as well as from guns on shore. Vietnamese Air Force planes attacked and sank the vessel. Government troops moved into the area and seized it after sharp combat with Viet Cong forces.

The ship, which had been sunk in shallow water, was fairly new and had been built in Communist China. It had already discharged a large cargo of weapons, ammunition, and other supplies for the Viet Cong. Documents found aboard the ship and on the bodies identified the vessel as having come from North Viet Nam. A newspaper in the cabin was from the North Vietnamese port city of Haiphong and was dated January 23, 1965. Also discovered were three North Vietnamese nautical charts, one of the Haiphong area and one of Hong Gay, both in North Viet Nam, and one of the Tra Vinh area of South Viet Nam. The military health records of North Vietnamese soldiers were found and a political background sheet of one man that showed he was a member of the 338th Division of the North Vietnamese Army.

Also aboard the Communist ship were an instruction book for a Chinese Communist navigational device, postcards and letters with addresses in North Viet Nam, and a number of photographs, including one of a group of uniformed North Vietnamese soldiers.

The capture of the Communist arms vessel caught North Viet Nam actually in the act of supplying arms to the Viet Cong in the South.

This had, of course, been long known, but here was proof. In sending the vessel down the South Vietnamese coast, the Communists had been either unduly sure of themselves—or desperate to get weapons to the Viet Cong.

At one time the Viet Cong had tried to conceal the source of arms provided to the terrorists in the South. In 1964, a secret document was captured from a Viet Cong agent. It had been sent from Viet Cong headquarters in Bien Hoa Province to subordinate units, and it ordered them to "pay special attention to the removal of all the markings and letters on weapons of all types currently employed by units and agencies and manufactured by friendly East European democratic countries or by China." The order said that every identifying marking should be chiseled off "so that the enemy cannot use it as a propaganda theme every time he captures these weapons."

Evidently there can be slip-ups even in organizations where errors are usually corrected by a shot in the back of the head, because in the vicinity of the captured Communist weapons ship were found five hundred pounds of medical supplies with labels from North Viet Nam, Communist China, Czechoslovakia, East Germany, the Soviet Union, and other places.

In addition, there were also:

> Approximately one million rounds of small arms ammunition

More than a thousand stick grenades

Five hundred pounds of TNT in prepared charges

Two thousand rounds of 82mm. mortar ammunition

Five hundred anti-tank grenades

Five hundred rounds of 57mm. recoilless rifle ammunition

More than a thousand rounds of 75mm. recoilless rifle ammunition

One 57mm. recoilless rifle

Two heavy machine guns

Two thousand 7.92mm. Mauser rifles

More than one hundred 7.62mm. carbines

One thousand submachine guns

Fifteen light machine guns

Five hundred rifles

This hardly came as a surprise to South Vietnamese officials, because North Viet Nam had consistently been pledging support to the Viet Cong, and marked weapons had frequently been captured. By some devious reasoning, however, the Communists appeared to feel that lip service to the cause would not lead to the deduction that material support was also being provided.

Communist China also has continually and publicly backed the Vietnamese Communists. On April 20, 1965, the Standing Committee of the Communist Chinese National People's Congress adopted a resolution declaring:

"The Chinese people have always resolutely supported the fraternal Vietnamese people in the joint struggle against U.S. imperialist aggression. Now, in the name of the 650,000,000 Chinese people, the Standing Committee of the National People's Congress solemnly declares that China will continue to do everything in its power to give resolute and unreserved support to the Vietnamese people in their patriotic and just struggle to resist U.S. aggression."

Behind the Viet Cong stand the North Vietnamese.

Behind the North Vietnamese stand the Communist Chinese.

To the Chinese, the war in Viet Nam is but a part of the world-wide struggle between Communism and the Free World. In Viet Nam the Chinese feel that, without having to use their own troops, and with a minimum material and financial outlay on their part, they can bog South Viet Nam down in a long, bloody, costly, and demoralizing campaign. As long as they can avoid direct involvement in the conflict, the Chinese have little to lose and a great deal to gain. If the Americans could be forced to leave, United States prestige would suffer around the world, and possibly all or most of Southeast Asia would fall under Chinese domination. If the American forces cannot be defeated, even so—the Chinese believe—the hard campaign will debilitate the United States and perhaps undermine its determination to defend other portions of the Free World from Communist encroachments.

The Chinese Communist leaders, having waged long guerrilla campaigns against the Japanese and the Chinese Nationalists, and having seen their tactics employed by Communists throughout Southeast Asia, are among the foremost proponents of that type of warfare in the world today. They believe that guerrilla warfare, effectively conducted, can defeat even a nuclear power like the United States.

One of the most important and revealing statements of Chinese Communist strategic thinking was contained in an article published on September 3, 1965, in *Renmin Ribao* (People's Daily). It was written by Lin Piao, Vice Premier, Minister of National Defense, and Vice Chairman of the Central Committee of the Communist Party of China, on the anniversary of the victory over Japan, and it dealt with that struggle and its lessons in detail. Lin wrote:

"Comrade Mao Tse-tung's theory of people's war . . . has not only been valid for China, it is a great contribution to the revolutionary struggles of the oppressed nations and peoples throughout the world. . . .

"The history of people's wars in China and other countries provides conclusive evidence that the growth of the people's revolutionary forces from

weak and small beginnings into strong and large
forces is a universal law of development of class
struggle, a universal law of development of people's war. A people's war inevitably meets with
many difficulties, with ups and downs and setbacks,
in the course of its development, but no force
can alter its general trend toward inevitable
triumph. . . .

"It must be emphasized that Comrade Mao Tse-
tung's theory of the establishment of rural revolutionary base areas and the encirclement of the
cities from the countryside is of outstanding and
universal practical importance for the present
revolutionary struggles of all the oppressed nations and peoples, and particularly for the revolutionary struggles of the oppressed nations and
peoples in Asia, Africa and Latin America against
imperialism and its lackeys. . . .

"Taking the entire globe, if North America and
Western Europe can be called 'the cities of the
world,' then Asia, Africa and Latin America con-
stitute 'the rural areas of the world.' Since World
War II, the proletarian revolutionary movement
has for various reasons been temporarily held back
in the North American and West European countries, while the people's revolutionary movement in
Asia, Africa and Latin America has been growing
vigorously. In a sense, the contemporary world
revolution also presents a picture of the encirclement of cities by the rural areas. In the final

analysis, the whole cause of world revolution hinges on the revolutionary struggles of the Asian, African and Latin American peoples who make up the overwhelming majority of the world's population. The socialist countries should regard it as their internationalist duty to support the people's revolutionary struggles in Asia, Africa and Latin America."

Red China's Vice Premier also declared, "At present, the main battlefield of the fierce struggle between the people of the world on the one side and U.S. imperialism and its lackeys on the other is the vast area of Asia, Africa and Latin America." In the Chinese view, all the world is a battlefield. Viet Nam is a segment of that battlefield, and, as the President of the United States, Lyndon Johnson, has said, "There are great stakes in the balance."

Chapter III

RURAL TERRORISM

News reports out of Saigon on the night of December 12, 1965, told of 23 Vietnamese civilians massacred by the Viet Cong. They were sprayed by machine gun fire as they slept. Seven others were critically wounded, and among the survivors was a three-year-old child, found under the dead body of its mother.

Their crime? They had been working on a canal for a small village south of Saigon. The Viet Cong did not want that canal built, and a finger on the trigger of a machine gun was their way of resolving the problem.

Reports such as these come out of Saigon every day. For terror as a tactic, according to Communist policy, starts in rural areas, surrounding and isolating the urban centers with a circle of hostile bases.

I flew from Saigon to My Tho, a busy town of 20,000 people situated on the banks of one of the main outlets of the Mekong River, to observe the effects of rural terrorism at first hand. This is rich delta land. From the air it is a patchwork of green vegetable gardens and brown, water-topped rice paddies quietly reflecting the scudding clouds overhead.

But the delta is also a war area, as most of South Viet Nam is a war area. Cars traveling along the road from the airport often carried sandbags to protect the passengers in the event that the vehicle ran over one of the mines which the Viet Cong like to plant by night.

I visited the areas around My Tho, and in each hamlet I heard accounts of Viet Cong incursions and of chiefs and villagers murdered or kidnapped. In front of one official house, cartridge shells were still strewn about the ground, reminders of a recent gun fight with Viet Cong raiders. In this area, the Viet Cong are usually no farther away than the nearest clump of trees—just across the road.

Rural terror is intended to serve fundamentally different strategic purposes from terror in the cities. In the latter, the Communists are basically seeking to undermine and discredit the government. In rural areas, tactics are aimed at gaining control over the populace, and then maintaining that control. Rural bases, maintained by Viet Cong threats of reprisals, are strategically important as

Their crime? Working on a canal for a small village south of Saigon. These are the bodies of some of the 23 canal workers murdered by the Viet Cong while they slept in a nearby pagoda.

Orphaned by the terrorist murder of the canal workers, this youngster is comforted by a Vietnamese soldier.

Coffins on a truck return the bodies of the murdered canal workers to their home provinces.

A woman and her children mourn for the workers shot down by Viet Cong because they were building a canal to increase the local rice crop.

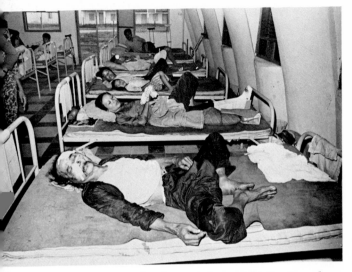

These are the survivors of a bus mining explosion two days before the New Lunar Year celebrations. The bus was filled with cheerful passengers on their way to join friends or families.

This woman's husband was killed in the bus mining explosion. She and her sons watch as the bodies are pulled from the wreckage.

This young man's wife and child will not be returning. They were on the bus. No identifiable parts of their bodies were found.

Viet Cong bombs killed or injured 89 Vietnamese as explosions ripped the My Canh floating restaurant in Saigon on the night of June 25, 1965. The restaurant and the quay are popular evening attractions for Vietnamese clerks and shopkeepers and children who enjoy the playground near the restaurant. Policemen and uninjured survivors assisted the wounded, whose faces reflect the shock and pain of their injuries.

An automobile burns fiercely after explosion of a Viet Cong bomb in the streets of Saigon.

A passer-by seeks aid for victims of a Saigon street explosion which killed 17 Vietnamese. Extensive damage was done to Vietnamese stores and homes in the area.

A bomb estimated to have contained 250 pounds of explosive killed eight Vietnamese and wounded 150 in Saigon. Many Vietnamese homes were also destroyed by the blast.

The body of a Saigon policeman lies crumpled against a wall where he was thrown by the force of a Viet Cong bomb which took 19 lives.

Village dwellers construct defenses for a "New Life Hamlet." These are guarded against Viet Cong guerrilla attacks by the inhabitants.

A member of the hamlet's Popular Force stands guard in his foxhole. The hamlet is ringed with barbed wire and mined moats.

Passes are checked before entering or leaving a village gate

A civil guardsman stands at his post in a watchtower at a village headquarters. The village radio is secured in this tower.

system of fixed and mobile checkpoints on land and water, day and night, deny the enemy access to vital logistics and communications routes. Private cars are frequently stopped and searched to prevent the transporting of weapons. Identification papers are examined in periodic census-taking, to be sure that "visitors" in villages and in Saigon are not Viet Cong infiltrators.

Railway workers repair a bridge destroyed by Viet Cong mines. Guerrillas constantly try to cut rail and road lines that supply the South Vietnamese Army. *UPI photo.*

Farmers and sheet metal workers are solving the problem of rice paddy irrigation by using outboard motors like those which power sampans and canal barges. This device for pumping water from a canal or pond is replacing the foot-pedaled waterwheels, baskets, and other laborious means.

At an agricultural training center this farmer has learned improved farming methods which he can apply without expensive tools or equipment.

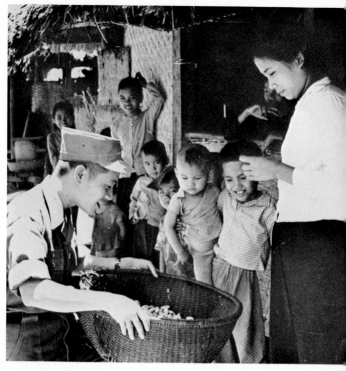

The girl in the white shirt was a Communist propagandist. She now works for the Vietnamese government. Here, she shows a basket of fruit her family has raised for market.

A young child, covered with sores and mosquito bites, is treated with antibiotic salve by a Vietnamese Army doctor during a stop at one of many villages visited.

Relief teams assist refugees who burned their village and their rice stocks to prevent their use by the Viet Cong. Vietnamese soldiers pass out clothing and supplies.

A Vietnamese Navy ship brings medical care. Here, a prescription is being filled for the child of a Vietnamese Junk Force sailor.

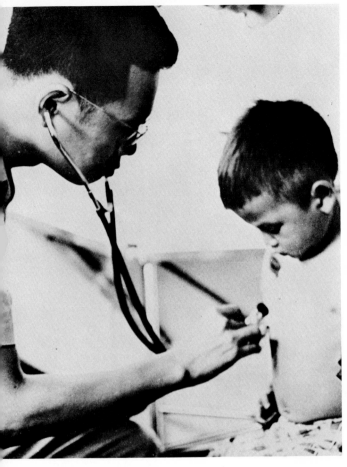

A Vietnamese Navy doctor examines a ticklish patient.

An exhibit of captured Communist-bloc arms taken from Viet
Cong terrorists in the South was held in Saigon by the Vietnamese Army. The arms, bearing markings from Communist
China and North Viet Nam, were undeniable evidence of
material support for the Viet Cong terrorists from Communist
countries to the north.

a source of food and as a means of concealment after marauding raids in the vicinity.

A man in fear of his life, or the lives of his wife and children, will be most reluctant to point out the guerrilla in his village or hamlet—a person who, clad in the traditional black pajamas and industriously tilling the rice paddies, is not distinguishable as the killer he becomes at nightfall. And the terrorizing of peasants in the countryside, where they do not have strong or well-organized police forces, is naturally easier than intimidating urban populations.

Since protection is the only ally the peasant has, the obvious way for the Viet Cong to win control is to destroy the government's presence and authority, which in the rural areas is represented and exercised by the hamlet and village chiefs and other local authorities. These, then, have been a primary target of the Viet Cong. Kill the hamlet chief and you destroy a great part of the control that the government maintains in a virtually isolated area. As the Viet Cong see it, if they kill an unpopular chief, they win the gratitude of the local people. If they kill a popular and strong chief, they eliminate an important enemy who stands in their way.

The Communists speak openly of their purpose. Truong Chinh, a high-ranking member of the North Vietnamese politburo, has demanded blunt-

ly: "Traitors to the nation, reactionaries and
enemies of the resistance must be immediately
eliminated."

Hoc Tap, a North Vietnamese publication,
stated in its July, 1964, issue: "The aim of the
revolution to liberate our compatriots in South
Viet Nam is to defeat the aggression and frustrate
the warmongering policies of the U.S. imperialists
and their lackeys. To that end it is necessary to
smash the reactionary administrative machinery
and the imperialists' mercenary army. This revolution can and should be settled only by the use
of revolutionary acts and the force of the masses
to defeat the enemy force; it absolutely cannot be
settled by laws and accords." Note the importance
given to smashing "administrative machinery."

Under such circumstances, asking a person to
become chief of a hamlet is virtually asking him
to sign his own death decree. Other types of government officials or workers in the provinces are
also high on the Viet Cong list, especially anyone
working on health conditions or highways or con-
structing public works in the villages—anyone
working for public improvement or law
enforcement.

It takes a brave man to be a chief or official in
the provinces. The fact that there are many such
brave men in South Vietnam is attested by the
fact that from January 1, 1965, to November 24
of the same year, 450 province, district, and ham-

let officials were killed and another 709 kidnapped. And, for each one murdered, maimed, or kidnapped, there was another ready to take his place.

The acts of terror aimed at undermining the governmental structure are directed not only at the local chiefs themselves, but also at their families. In Binh Dinh Province, the Viet Cong beheaded a village chief and cut off an arm of his twelve-year-old daughter. They took the chief's six-year-old son, laid a rifle across his bare back and fired it several times, leaving a long scar.

Barbarism, yes; but not necessarily barbarism for the sake of barbarism. It is brutality with a purpose. A strong man is needed as a local chief in Viet Nam these days. And strong men can be killed, too. And their families.

But the murder of local chiefs is only one prong of the Communist terror tactics in rural areas. Another merciless prong is directed against local inhabitants. Again there is purpose behind the ruthlessness: to intimidate the citizenry, to discredit the government's ability to protect the people, to make possible Viet Cong collection of "taxes" and recruitment of men, and to assure, if not popular support, at least that frightened citizens will not reveal to government forces the identities or hiding places of Viet Cong members.

Almost routine are newspaper reports such as one carried in the September 24, 1965 issue of *The Saigon Post*:

"SAIGON, *Sept. 23* (VP) The Viet Cong were intensifying their crimes against civilian population in various provinces.

"In Kien Hoa, they exploded a mine on Tuesday morning, in Tam Phuoc village's Tan Ninh hamlet, killing six persons including four schoolboys.

"According to local residents, Tam Phuoc village's police chief Nguyen Van Ngoc and militiaman Ha Van Hoi that morning made an inspection tour of the hamlet upon learning the news that VC leaflets were scattering around the area. While they were just about 200 meters from the local school, the VC exploded a mine which killed instantly both of them. Four schoolboys—Nguyen Van Con, 11, Le Van Dien, 11, Nguyen Van Le, 9, and Phan Minh Khai, 10—who happened to pass by were also hit by the explosion and died on the spot.

"In a pursuit operation afterwards, the Tam Phuoc Militia confiscated a second 25-kilo mine left by the terrorists.

"Two days earlier, in Dinh Tuong province, an armed group of VC broke into the Phong Thuan hamlet at about 3 a.m. and stabbed to death Mr. Huynh Van Trinh, 33, the local health official.

"A few minutes later, they called on Mr. Tran Van Phan, a local farmer, and asked for taxes. As the latter did not comply with their orders, they also killed him on the spot.

"Also in Dinh Tuong, the VC kidnapped Mr. Le Nhu Que of An Huu village last Sept. 16 and led him to the Rach Gia Mieng area where the victim was shot dead.

"Meanwhile, four Viet Cong disguised as farmers last Sept. 14 boated to the My Long market in Kien Hoa's Giong Trom district. Immediately after their landing they killed two local residents who recognized them and tried to sound the alarm.

"At the same time, a group of Communists ambushing on the other bank opened fire into the market to cover their four accomplices' retreat.

"The large crowd at the market fled in panic but no casualties were reported.

"In Phuoc Long province, the VC raided last Sept. 10 Phuoc Tin village's Catholic church where they smashed down statues and portraits at the altar, and destroyed many houses of local residents who had refused to pay taxes to them."

The South Vietnamese Government, in white papers and in protests to the International Control Commission set up by the 1954 Geneva Agreement, has repeatedly recorded Communist terror tactics over the years. A report to the Commission in February of 1962 stated:

"On January 15, 1962 at about 1800 hours, a Viet-Cong squad armed with cutlasses descended upon the hamlet of Phu-Van, Phu-Hoa village, Chau-Thanh district, Binh-Duong province, and

seized Miss Pham-Thi-Doi, also known as Giau, of
the Republican Youth of that village. They carried Miss Doi to a place—and savagely murdered
her.

"The victim was found with her hands tied behind her back, her head and her right arm com-
pletely cut off, and the body showing deep and
numerous gashes made in cold blood. The mur-
derers left on the body a death sentence accusing
her of working for the Security Service of
Phu-Loi."

A South Vietnamese white paper issued in 1963
reported the following incidents:

"On July 5, 1962, the Misses Tran-Thi-Bong,
16, and Tran-Thi-Loan, 19, members of the Cong-
Hoa Youth of Binh-Dac hamlet, Son-Chau village, Quang-Ngai province, were kidnapped and
buried alive by armed Viet-Cong. It is a miracle
that these two young girls succeeded in freeing
themselves, after super-human efforts, by scooping
out an opening in the sandy soil with their bare
hands. . . .

"On December 19, 1962, Viet-Cong terrorists
entered the church at Ngoc-Kinh, 60 kilometers
West of Hoi-An (Quang-Nam Province) and assassi-
nated the Reverend Father Nguyen-Huu-Ngoi and
Mr. Phan-Hau, a member of the Community Council of Loc-Vinh."

In a 1964 white paper, the South Vietnamese
Government reported additional incidents:

"The assassination by some twenty Viet-Cong

of Mr. Ngo-Tien, aged 58, a councillor of Phu-Hai hamlet (Thua-Thien Province) at about 8:00 p.m. on January 19th, 1964, 400 yards from his house. A bill of indictment was discovered on the victim's body.

"Mr. Nguyen-Phuoc-Dang from Phu-Tuan village in the Binh-Dai district of Kien-Hoa Province was decapitated by the Viet-Cong on the night of October 1st/2nd, 1963. A written sentence of death was likewise pinned to the victim's body."

The mining of roads, the machine-gunning of buses, the kidnapping of civilians, the burning of homes, the use of torture and murder—all of these are weapons in the Communist arsenal of terror, all are employed in the ruthless campaign to break the resistance of the citizenry. And in carrying out this campaign, the Viet Cong miss no opportunity, spare no target. In November of 1964 Viet Nam was hard hit by typhoons and rains. As rescue operations were under way, the Viet Cong fired at people crossing a river to higher ground and repeatedly shot at helicopters evacuating storm victims. They ambushed three trucks carrying relief supplies, killing three relief workers, wounding six, and kidnapping five others.

Captured Viet Cong and defectors from the Viet Cong ranks have, under questioning, spoken openly about the Communist terror tactics. Their replies show the mindless reaction and the robot-like obedience to orders which their terrorist masters have instilled in them.

A twenty-seven-year-old soldier who defected in Binh Long Province gave this account:

Q. Have you seen terrorist actions?

A. I saw five men killed by the [National Liberation] Front during the attacks on strategic hamlets: four policemen and the hamlet chief of Phu Mieng.

Q. Why were they killed?

A. Because they were refractory people. When a Government official was reported as a secret policeman, as being rude to the people or as an extortionist we would throw a letter into his house at night asking him to change his ways and to resign his position. He was warned only once. If he continued to be arrogant he would be considered to be refractory, and when the hamlet was taken by the Front force and the people gathered together, the refractory policeman would be led in front of the people, the verdict of the People's Tribunal would be read aloud and then the sentence would be carried out by firing or by beheading.

Q. What was the People's Tribunal?

A. I do not know. It must have been decided that the man had to die. On the day of the execution, the VC cadre member read to the people the sentence of the Tribunal, which went like this: "On such day this man committed such crime, etc. Despite our warning he has shown himself to be refractory and he has continued his evil deeds which are such-and-such. After deliberation the People's Tribunal has found him guilty of crimes against the people and has sentenced him to death." After he was shot, the decision of the People's Tribunal was fastened to his stomach as a warning to others not to commit the same misdeeds.

Another military defector, twenty-six years old and a member of the party, told of the methods used to force citizens to pay Viet Cong taxes:

Q. Have you seen or engaged in acts of terrorism?

A. Yes, this usually happened when the villagers would not pay taxes to the Front. In May, 1964, we had to kill two villagers because they refused to pay taxes to the Front. In all we killed about forty of them.

Q. What kind of people were they?

A. Some were old; some young. They belonged to the group of landowners and they refused to pay.

Q. Who gave orders to kill them?

A. I received instructions from the District [headquarters] to kill anybody who would stand against the Front by refusing to pay Front taxes.

Q. How did you feel about these killings?

A. I thought that the cruelest thing to do was to kill a man who had a wife and children. Now I feel very sorry.

Q. If they refused to pay taxes to the Front, did you kill them right away?

A. I received orders from the Front to kill

them. I did not kill them the first time they refused
to pay, but first I warned them three times before
my men killed them. In these warnings we made
threats or we covered their eyes with a cloth.

Q. What were the results of these warnings?

A. In spite of the warnings and threats, these
people often refused to pay.

One twenty-year-old hard-core Viet Cong who
defected in mid-1964 in Phuoc Tuy clearly showed
the effects of Communist brainwashing in regard
to terror tactics—even explaining away the beheading of his father by the Viet Cong. He told why
he had defected: "Before I joined the Revolution,
I was told that by joining the Revolution I would
fight for my family first and then for myself. But
I realized that my family had not benefited from
the fighting and on the contrary had suffered from
the Revolution by losing half of its land. For myself I was bored with life with the Front, because
I had to work all day long with no rest at all. The
fighting has lasted too long for me, and I have not
improved my situation at all. When peace comes
at last, I would still have to work with my hoe and
my plough. I would have no profession at all."

The defector lived in a government-controlled
area at the time his father was murdered by the
Viet Cong in 1959. He related: "I was not at home
when my father was killed. I came home at 11
P.M. My father had been killed at about 9 P.M. He

was beheaded in front of the house with a sword. The Viet Cong left behind the verdict of the People's Court saying that my father was a tyrannical hamlet chief; that he had perpetrated bloody crimes against the people; that he had exploited the people; and so he had to pay for his crimes. My first thought was that he was innocent and that he was the victim of a plot by someone who hated him. But then I guessed that he must have committed some crime. Otherwise he would not have been beheaded. He would only have been asked by the Viet Cong to resign his position, just as other people who worked for the Government and had not perpetrated any crime against the people.

"After the killing, the VC came often to my house to educate me. They analyzed my father's crimes. They said my father was a lackey paid by the enemy to harm the people. They said a lot of things; I cannot remember them all. Thereafter I had no more hatred for the VC because my father was guilty and had to pay for his crimes, I did not believe in his innocence any more and I forgot about his death."

Eight months after the killing, the indoctrinated youth joined the Viet Cong. Questioned after his defection he gave the following justification for his previous actions:

Q. What did you think of the Front's terrorist operations?

A. We terrorized and murdered only those who

worked for the Government. If they refused to resign their position when asked to by the VC, or if they were found guilty of crimes against the people, they were classified as refractory elements and executed.

Q. Did you witness other types of terrorist actions?

A. Yes, all the time, things such as the burning of strategic hamlets, the mining of bridges, the stopping of buses.

Q. Did you participate in these terrorist actions?

A. Yes. I killed four spies in 1960 in Loc Thuan. I cut their heads off so as not to waste bullets. When I joined the [VC] Main Force I did not have to carry out these terroristic actions. They were left to the local men.

Q. What did you think of the murder of civilians?

A. Those men were not civilians, but lackeys of the enemy and harmful to the aspirations of the people. It was the duty of the benefactors of the people to get rid of those men.

Q. Who gave the order to execute them?

A. The District Committee.

Documents captured from the Viet Cong reflect the same ruthless attitude toward executions, the pretense that these are carried out for the good of the citizenry. Viet Cong reports boast of "capturing a tyrant" or that " a cruel hamlet chief was killed." The names of persons "to be liquidated" are listed, and these are tagged as: a "policeman," an "informant," an "adjutant," "puppet army personnel."

There were 19,227 Communist acts of terrorism in South Viet Nam during 1964, according to the official record, and there is no way of knowing how many may have escaped official attention. Among those recorded, 1359 civilians were killed, 1970 were wounded, and 8423 were kidnapped. But cold statistics do not indicate the viciousness of the Communist attacks nor the human tragedies involved in each case.

On Sunday, November 15, 1964, while worshipers were attending Mass in the Suoi Giai church of Phuoc Thanh Province, Viet Cong terrorists launched an attack against the church with 60mm. mortars and grenade launchers. Four people were killed and nine others wounded.

The brutality continued unabated in 1965. The Viet Cong entered Hoa Hoi Hamlet in Binh Dinh Province and burned 185 civilian homes. In Long An Province, Viet Cong mines blew up three buses, killing eleven civilians. In Pleiku Province, a Viet Cong company took over a hamlet and murdered ten members of the council. A Viet Cong platoon entered Phu Long Hamlet in Binh Thuan Province and killed an old man and raped two women. The Viet Cong stopped buses in Thua Thien Province and kidnapped a nurse and two girls. Also in Pleiku, a bus was fired upon. The driver was killed and ten passengers wounded.

Foreigners were not exempt from Viet Cong brutality. A captured Swiss cameraman was tortured and killed. Three American soldiers who were captured were disemboweled and emasculated.

The number of incidents in 1964 was almost double that of 1963. One reason for the increase was a change in Viet Cong tactics. Previously, terror had been carried out on a largely selective basis, i.e., it was aimed at special individuals, such as village chiefs. But in 1964 the Viet Cong broadened their tactics and vastly increased their indiscriminate techniques. Thus, a mine planted under a country road would kill a large number of people —people not specifically targeted by the Viet Cong but unlucky enough to be near the explosion.

Several explanations have been offered as the reasons for the change in Communist tactics. One of the primary reasons, evidently, was a sense of desperation in the face of increasing American involvement in the Vietnamese struggle. The Viet Cong may have hoped for quick victory through an all-out military and terror campaign before the United States forces grew too big to be defeated. Another reason for the Viet Cong tactical change may well have been their failure to win general support in the countryside. In the early years, the Viet Cong may have refrained from machine-gunning buses in order not to antagonize the local populace. Later, however, having failed to win popular support, the Viet Cong broadened its terror tactics in an effort to frighten the people into submission.

Choosing at random a five-day period, from August 19 through August 23, 1965, Communist terror incidents in the countryside included: mining a hamlet information office; murdering the Xuan Thoi Thuong hamlet chief; throwing a grenade at a police station; detonating a mine that damaged a civilian bus and wounded nine people; firing on a police team on a traffic control mission (one civilian was killed); kidnapping several youths; confiscating four motorized junks from wood cutters, thus depriving them of their means of livelihood; mining and damaging rails on a bridge.

These are only a sampling of the incidents that occurred during this single period. In some instances, the results were serious; in others, the victims suffered only harassment. But this attrition has continued in South Viet for more than eight years without letup and it has been accompanied by a full-scale war.

It has been an acid test for the national soul, and it is to the highest credit of the Vietnamese people that their nation did not crumble into chaos long ago. But terror is not the ultimate weapon and it does not automatically bring victory. It is even debatable whether terror may have done the Viet Cong more harm than good.

There were an estimated six hundred thousand refugees in South Viet Nam in September, 1965, and the majority had come from Viet Cong–controlled territory. The war raging around them was the reason the refugees had fled. But an additional factor was the terror-pressure tactics applied by the Viet Cong against the populace: rapidly rising taxation, impressment of youths into the Communist forces, forced attendance at frequent propaganda meetings, the police surveillance which is a part of every Communist state. And the inevitable executions.

An old man, a refugee, said: "The VC executed four persons in my village. They explained that these people were paid agents of the Government authorities: Nobody could figure out whether this was true or not. Everybody was afraid. No one dared say anything."

A farmer stated: "Some twenty people were carried away from my village. One didn't know where. Six people were killed: a hamlet chief, and those who had relatives working in the Vietnamese Army, as well as the Village Council members. Their throats were cut. In 1962 the VC killed in the same way two men whom they suspected of having participated in the repair of the road leading from Ba Beo to the pagoda.

"Many people were unhappy but they dared not

speak out. Once a woman went to the My Tho
market to sell her ducks and chickens to the Government people and, upon her return to the village, she was arrested, then killed. She was accused
of supplying the Government."

Terrorism frightens the populace, but it does
not subdue them. There are indications that the
constant brutality is counter-productive in another
way, adversely affecting the morale of Viet Cong
members themselves.

One Viet Cong who defected in May of 1965
was a South Vietnamese who had gone to North
Viet Nam and then.been infiltrated south again.
He was an important defector, having been a party
member as well as political officer of his Viet Cong
unit. He told why he had defected and how he
had saved the family of a citizen named Cai:

"I was dissatisfied because the VC killed innocent people and did many things which hurt my
conscience. I was very afraid while I stayed with
them, but I was shrewd and my high rank helped
a lot. I was a political officer, and the District
Chief himself could only advise me; he could not
give orders to me. I was very zealous and authori-
tative. Whenever I came into a village, I was
treated with meat and the best rice.

"If the District Chief had been a smart fellow
he would have noticed that I was definitely against
them as early as the time I failed to arrest Cai's
family. He told me to go and arrest Cai's family

—his father, his wife and his two sisters. But that night I pondered on it. Because I had my mind set on returning to live with my family and with the Vietnamese Government, I decided to save Cai's family.

"I started to work on [Viet Cong Member] Quang who was to lead the operation. I told him: 'You are sick today, you had better stay here. I will lead the operation for you.' I went on and said: 'I have received word that the Government forces are carrying out an operation down there.' He was scared. Then I went to meet the District Chief. I said to him: 'Quang is sick today, and besides I think it will be difficult to carry out that mission. May I suggest that you let me take charge of it? I will tell Cai to give us some rice, and if he refuses I will blow out his brains.' The District Chief was interested in my idea and let me go.

"First I had Mr. Cau, Cai's father, give me two bags of rice, and then I whispered to him: 'To-morrow night you had better stay in the District town. Take Cai's wife with you and have his two sisters sleep elsewhere in the village, because I will come back tomorrow to shoot you.' Tears came to his eyes and he thanked me.

"The following night we crossed the river by sampan, and I kicked open the door of Mr. Cau's house and began to fire with my pistol. I fired three times. Everybody fled, thinking it was an ambush. I kicked the furniture and I swore aloud. The District Chief came to inquire about the racket I had made. I told him that Cau had fled. He said: 'Your shooting has scared the population.' I said: 'I don't care. It is the only way to act toward the traitor. Where can he be?' I met one of Cai's sisters the next day and told her to go and put some order inside the house. She said: 'I am alive thanks to you. I don't care about the disorder even if you have set the house on fire.' "

This same defector frankly told of Viet Cong killings. "The VC pinned an accusation on the chests of the victims they executed. They did that to scare the people, because actually the victims had committed no crimes. But the VC killed them none-the-less and invented all kinds of crimes that the victims had supposedly committed. They did that to show the people that the innocent-looking victims had actually committed the most horrible crimes.

"Thus, sons came to applaud the execution of their fathers. This is proof of how effective the VC propaganda was. Sons applauded because they thought they were lucky their fathers had been killed before they could kill their own sons. The sons were saved thanks to the clearsightedness of the Party. They did not notice that their fathers could not defend themselves against the accusations because they were already dead."

A poem, found on the body of a North Vietna-

mese soldier killed at Duc Co, gave eloquent voice
to the youth's feelings. The poem, addressed to his
mother, Mrs. Tran Thi Phan, was as follows:

From the day I left you, O Mother,
To follow my companions in this trip through
    Laos to Central Viet Nam,
I have endured the hardships of climbing the
    green mountains
And marching through rain and shine. . . .
Here I am, on strangers' soil,
But the South is also my country. . . .
I began to look around and wondered what
    there was here to liberate.
The market was crowded with people in
    gay mood,
The rice fields were green with rice plants.
From a curve-roofed pagoda came the sound
    of a worship bell.
The classrooms were full of cheerful children
Singing a song in chorus.
And in a plot of garden the small butterflies
    were busy
On the yellow cabbage flowers.
Peace and joy reigned throughout the country.
But why had they ordered me to burn the
    villages, destroy the bridges
Lay mines to sow death around?
Often my hands trembled
While laying a mine, because later on I saw

People blown up and blood sprayed around.
Whose blood was it?
It was the blood of our people, those like
    Mother and me.
That night, my eyes were filled with tears
And my sleep with nightmares.

For the people of South Viet Nam, there have
been eight years of nightmares, and the end is not
yet in sight.

Chapter IV

URBAN TERRORISM

How can you tell a terrorist when you see one? That young man admiring the goods in a shop window? Is he one? Or that dignified gentleman sipping a mid-morning coffee in a sidewalk café? Is he? Or the frail shoeshine boy with the friendly grin? Who knows—until too late. And then he fades into the panic-stricken crowd and is gone— a faceless weapon of Communist underground movements in the urban areas.

Terrorists in the cities are considered by the Communists as "urban guerrillas," and their tactics are basically the same as those in the countryside —to hit and run. Their purpose is to discredit and weaken the established government by bombings, to discourage business activity, cause investment capital to flee, and in general, to undermine the economy. The people—the Communists believe— will become convinced of the strength of the Viet Cong and lose faith in the ability of the government to protect them. The government will lose support, and there will be a yearning for peace, even on Communist terms.

Such a deduction is ridiculous to any rational person. After being a witness, or a victim, of such displays of Communist tactics, who would do anything but resist with his utmost strength the possibility of being drawn under such influence? But then, we are not talking about rational people when we speak of such cause-and-effect reasoning —we are talking about minds that have been warped by Communist training and tactics. They have no compunction about killing countless innocent Vietnamese civilian countrymen to gain their objective of domination.

One would hardly see anything for the Communists to boast about in the My Canh floating restaurant tragedy on June 25, 1965, but boast they did. North Viet Nam's Radio Hanoi acclaimed ". . . A great number of killed and wounded U. S. aggressors were found and carried from the restaurant. Morever, many dead bodies of the aggressors were buried under the tables and chairs and debris of the restaurant. . . ."

The actual fact was that out of the 124 casualties, 28 were American. The remainder—Vietnamese fellow countrymen.

Other comments by Radio Hanoi: "Let us acclaim this great victory by the Saigon armed forces. . . ." And, "The South Vietnamese people and our compatriots are overjoyed at this feat of arms. . . ."

The Communists might have been overjoyed, but it is doubtful if the survivors agreed.

Q. What is your name, my boy, and how old are you?

A. My name is Le Trong Toan. I am thirteen years old.

Q. Do you have parents, and where do they live?

A. Yes, I have parents. They live in Thi Nghe.

Q. What were you doing at the Bach Dang Quay at that time?

A. I was selling peanuts.

Q. How many wounds do you have?

A. Two places, on my back and on my leg.

Q. Did you have any surgery?

A. Yes, to take the shrapnel out.

Q. How do you feel now?

A. A little better.

Another survivor, a paint seller, reported the episode:

Q. What is your name and profession?

A. My name is Mai Van Nhan. I am seventeen years old and I am a paint retailer.

Q. Could you tell us about the explosion that injured you?

A. I was having some refreshment right at the phone station. I was looking at the water when there was the explosion behind my back. I was wounded right after the first blast. My head went down and I saw my blood spilling out.

Q. Where were you wounded?

A. On my head, my leg and my buttock—shrapnel, I guess.

The mother of a girl killed on the My Canh was also interviewed:

Q. What is your name and profession, please?

A. My name is To Thi My. I am in business. Phuong Thao is my daughter.

Q. At the time of the explosion at the My Canh Restaurant, was Phuong Thao [a professional singer] entertaining customers there?

A. No, she was dining there with some of her friends. They were there just for a good time.

Q. How old was Phuong Thao?

A. She was twenty-two years old.

The record of Communist terrorism in Saigon is long and murderous. During the past twenty years the people of that city have known little respite from attacks. Terror has become so much a part of the scene that virtually every bar, hotel, and restaurant has permanent iron grates of metal screening to protect the patrons from tossed grenades.

The attacks diminished for a time after 1949, due to improved French security and to the breaking away of non-Communist nationalists from the

Viet Minh. In 1954 after the Geneva Agreements were signed, Saigon entered a period of comparative tranquillity.

In the late 1950's when the Communists began their campaign to conquer South Vietnam, a new city terror campaign also began. It has never stopped since then. Thousands of grenades have been thrown and thousands of bombs exploded, taking a tragic toll. On October 26, 1962, a grenade was thrown into a crowd attending a Vietnamese Air Force fair being held in front of Saigon's City Hall. Seven Vietnamese were killed and forty-five were injured.

During 1965 there were several major terror attacks. Among them were the following:

On March 3, a bomb was discovered at midnight in the Mayflower Bar. A doorboy picked it up and was carrying it away when it exploded, killing the boy as well as three other children. A man and four additional children were injured.

On March 30 a car drove toward the U. S. Embassy and then stopped, apparently due to engine trouble. One of three policemen on guard came over and ordered the occupants to move the vehicle. They said they were unable to do so. Suddenly, a nearby Viet Cong on a motorcycle opened fire on the policeman. He fired back, and the men in the car also began shooting, as they attempted to escape. With a thunderous roar, the car exploded; the blast smashed a wide area. The Em-

bassy and other buildings were damaged, and
bodies were strewn about the streets. Twenty-two
people were killed, including one of the terrorists
and two Americans. One hundred and eighty-eight
people were injured.

On June 16, an explosion rocked the main lobby
of Tan Son Nhut Airport. Thirty-six people of
various nationalities were injured.

On October 3, a blast occured at 1:15 in the
afternoon outside Cong Hoa Stadium, where
policemen had been going through training exer-
cises. Nine persons—five policemen and four children—were killed, and thirty-two persons were
injured. A second explosive device, discovered concealed in a basket of vegetables, was dismantled.
Another explosion occurred later in the day at
another place in the city. A bomb or grenade being transported in a taxi exploded, apparently pre-
maturely. Two people were killed and ten others
injured.

The following table provides a statistical picture
of Viet Cong terrorism in Saigon from 1961 to
1965:

	1961	1962	1963	1964	9 mos. of 1965
Number of incidents	11	14	33	57	55
Persons killed	6	7	18	16	79
Persons injured	18	61	133	350	450

At times the Viet Cong attacks have been directed at special targets, such as Americans or policemen. But the Viet Cong have not been particularly careful in placing their explosives, and invariably Vietnamese citizens number first among the victims. The above table includes victims of all nationalities. Of the total of 126 deaths, 24 were Americans, and the rest were chiefly Vietnamese.

On August 24, 1964, a well-dressed Viet Cong registered under a false name at Saigon's Caravelle Hotel. He was given a room on the fifth floor. The following day he left the hotel, and a few minutes later an explosion rocked the building. The Caravelle is one of Saigon's international spots, and the Viet Cong were evidently hoping to kill Americans. No Americans were killed or injured. However, one Frenchman, one New Zealander, and more than a dozen Vietnamese were wounded.

Viet Cong callousness and disregard for the lives of innocent people were demonstrated in the questioning of a captured Viet Cong saboteur. He provided the following first-hand account:

Q. Tell us of your activities.

A. On January 27, 1965, Bay [a fellow Viet Cong] called at my place to tell me that he had received orders to blow up the Bamboo Bar on Vo Tanh Street, Gia Dinh, on January 30. The bar was frequented by Americans. A couple of days later Bay called again and gave me 300 piasters.

This was a sort of bonus from the Front. The next day, that is, on January 30, he brought a pistol and a big lump of plastic wrapped in paper. He arrived around seven p. m. on a motorcycle, entered my house and put the plastic on the table. Bay outlined his plan of operation and told me what I had to do. At 8:30 p.m. he began preparing the plastic. I went outside in the yard and started my "mobylette." All of a sudden the plastic exploded, and it threw me to the ground. I was unconscious. Later, when I recovered consciousness, I found myself at Cho Ray Hospital. It was at that moment that an attendant told me that the explosion had killed three persons. I learned that my mother and sister had been killed at the same time as Bay. They were in an adjoining room, but my father was out.

Q. What were your plans to blow up the Bamboo Bar?

A. There's a Chinese soup shop next to the Bamboo Bar, separated from it by a thin partition. Bay was supposed to go there and pretend to buy soup. He was to avail himself of the occasion to place the plastic on a little table against the partition. Meanwhile, I was to protect him during the operation. I had a pistol on me and was to follow about twenty meters behind him. Should police or security agents try to arrest him, I was to shoot them to help Bay escape. While he was inside the soup shop I was to stay outside to keep watch, seeming to adjust something on my motorbike. Once he had succeeded in placing the plastic and had left the shop, we were to separate without a word to each other.

Q. What was the purpose of blowing up the Bamboo Bar?

A. The place was frequented by Americans only. The purpose was to kill them.

Q. Why did you want to kill them?

A. According to our cadres [officers] it was a way of carrying out the order to drive them out of the country.

Q. When you agreed to carry out this mission, did you think of the other people besides the Americans in the soup shop and the bar who might have been killed by the explosion?

A. I had thought of that and had even suggested to Bay that he place the plastic inside the bar to avoid killing the people in the soup shop. But he said there was no way of placing the plastic in the bar and that it was an order to be executed without delay.

The Viet Cong underground in the Saigon area is established along the typical lines of a Communist organization. At the bottom are the cells, and a member of one cell does not know the members of other cells—or sometimes even other members

of his own cell. At the top of the organization—
but under the so-called National Liberation Front
—is the *Dac Khu Uy Saigon Cholon Giadinh,* or
Special Saigon–Cholon–Gia-Dinh Zonal Committee. Cholon is a Chinese area adjoining Saigon,
and Gia Dinh is the province in which Saigon is
located.

The Zonal Committee has jurisdiction over all
of Gia Dinh, as well as portions of four adjoining
provinces. At the head of the Committee is a
chairman, and under him are the deputy chairman, secretary-general, and commissars for certain
activities, such as finances and military affairs. The
area under the Committee has been divided into
three "provinces": northern, southern, and Saigon
proper.

Within the urban area, Saigon and adjoining
sections, the clandestine Viet Cong apparatus consists of three operational units. These are C. (Company) 159, Unit 65, and Unit 67. The Viet Cong
call these *dac cong* units: *dac cong* means "special
action," which is a euphemism for terrorism.

C. 159 has about 250 members, and each of the
other units has between 150 and 200 men. This
means that the Viet Cong have over 500 people
dedicated to the spreading of death and terror
in the capital of South Viet Nam.

The actual organization of Unit 65 is as follows:

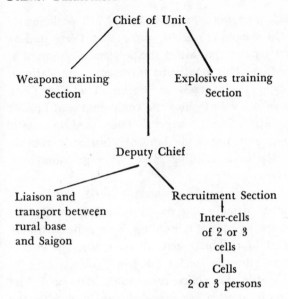

Orders can be passed down the chain of command, Zonal Committee to chief of special action unit to inter-cell chief, but members of cells need not know what other cells are doing, or even who their members are. The police may round up the members of a cell, but breaking up a network is exceedingly difficult.

Terrorism as a policy is directed at first one Saigon group and then another, usually in proportion to the threat that each presents to Communist objectives. It is evident that the effectiveness of the police has been causing considerable worry and inconvenience to the terrorist during

1965. The word has gone out—"Kill policemen!"

On August 16, 1965, three Viet Cong passing in a car shot and killed the policeman on guard at the Cong Hoa Boulevard entrance to the National Police Headquarters in Saigon. The Viet Cong drove the vehicle into the compound and opened fire with several weapons. They used automatic arms, and a grenade launcher hurled a grenade on top of a building. Two other grenades were thrown.

A plastic bomb—estimated at 60 pounds—exploded, demolishing six jeeps and approximately 100 feet of wall of a building. Two policemen were killed in the blast and six were injured, one of whom later died of his wounds.

Outside the police compound, additional Viet Cong in another car provided covering fire for the attackers with smoke bombs and automatic weapons.

After the assault, all of the Viet Cong escaped in the waiting car. In the course of their escape, they shot and killed a traffic policeman on Truong Van Le Street.

The toll for the deed: five policemen killed, five wounded.

The Viet Cong began their systematic campaign against policemen during 1965.* The campaign

---

* Communist tactics often follow a world-wide pattern. Communist militants, during the 1965 uprising in the Dominican Republic, also carried out a campaign to slay as

has two purposes. First, the police represent and exercise the authority of the national government. To hurt the police is to damage the government's power and authority. Second, police, particularly in Saigon, have become increasingly effective in countering Viet Cong activities. The Viet Cong are striking back in an attempt to demoralize the police and lessen their effectiveness. On March 1, 1965, an explosive charge hit a police firing range. Two policemen were killed and thirty-three persons were injured, including twenty-six other policemen. On June 10, 1965, another charge was fired at the Third Police Precinct. One policeman and two civilians were killed, and eighteen civilians were injured.

During 1964, nine policemen were injured in four incidents aimed directly at police in Saigon. But during the first nine months of 1965 there were sixteen incidents directed against the Saigon police, resulting in the death of eight policemen and the wounding of fifty-two.

Throughout South Viet Nam, Viet Cong activities caused the following police casualties during the first eight months of 1965:

---

many policemen as possible. An article by Lenin, "Partisan Warfare," published in 1906, stated, "to kill individuals such as high officials and lower-ranking members of the police and army" is an objective of revolutionary armed struggle.

	Killed in action	Wounded in action	Missing	Captured
January	11	47	2	2
February	19	9	4	0
March	33	23	12	0
April	19	14	8	0
May	15	49	0	3
June	17	32	8	0
July	27	40	15	0
August	10	0	12	0

Some of the casualties resulted from military activities, and were not necessarily a part of the anti-police terror campaign, but the greater portion of the casualties were due directly to the campaign.

A typical incident occurred late in September of 1965. A plane crashed, or was shot down at Bao Tri, about fifty miles south of Saigon, and the three American civilians aboard were killed. Seven Vietnamese policemen were sent to guard the crash site. The Viet Cong attacked the site and killed all of the policemen.

The following is a sampling of incidents involving police during the months of August and September, 1965:

A police squad patrolling on Route 13 in Binh Duong Province on August 5 was attacked by a squad of Viet Cong, who detonated a Claymore-type mine, killing one policeman and injuring another. The police counterattacked and the Viet

Cong withdrew. A second mine and two rolls of wire were captured, as well as a typewritten leaflet calling on Vietnamese police to join the Viet Cong and turn against the United States forces.

The Viet Cong fired at and wounded two Saigon policemen on August 14 while the police were searching a passer-by at the intersection of Le Dai Hanh and Duong Cong Trung streets.

The Viet Cong tossed a grenade into the Tran Van Thinh subprecinct station in Saigon on August 20, wounding four policemen and fifteen civilians.

A jeep attached to the Nguyen Van Bac sub-station in Saigon was attacked on August 28 on Tan That Thuyet Street. Two grenades were thrown at the vehicle, but each missed its target and failed to explode.

The anti-police terror campaign was by no means confined to Saigon. Provincial police were also being singled out for special attention. The following is a sampling of actions taken against them during the same period of August and September, 1965:

The police headquarters in Long Dien District, Phuoc Tuy Province, was attacked at 2:15 A.M. on August 13. The district police chief and two other policemen were killed, and another police-man was wounded. The attack was repulsed and the Viet Cong withdrew. Two Viet Cong dead and one wounded were left behind, and one was captured.

The Viet Cong attempted to assassinate a village policeman in Bien Hoa Province on August 25. He managed to escape with slight wounds.

During the first ten days of September, a total of six policemen were killed by the Viet Cong in An Xuyen Province, including the district police chief of Thoi Binh. Seven other policemen were wounded and one was missing. In one incident, the Viet Cong attacked the police station in Thoi Binh District on September 1. The Communists used 60 and 81mm. mortars, machine guns, recoilless rifles, and other weapons. Four policemen were killed and four others wounded.

In the cities, as in the villages, the Vietnamese live hourly with death—be they public officials or simple workers. They remain stubbornly unconvinced that they are being "liberated" Viet Cong style into a better way of life by their murdering fellow countrymen.

Chapter V

ANSWERS TO TERROR

How does one fight an enemy one cannot see, cannot find because he wears no uniform or identification, and who disappears the moment after he has struck?

There are several ways, in addition to military might, and they are all being used with increasing effectiveness by the Vietnamese police and civilian population. These brave people are assisted and advised by their Allies, 27 Free World nations as well as the United States.

Psychological warfare and civilian self-help activities are the two answers producing the positive results that are easiest to see and to evaluate.

Vietnamese civilian and military organizations, together with their Allies, cooperate in the psychological warfare effort. In one sense, it is turning their own tactics back onto the Viet Cong— but without the bombs and beheadings. Many of the Viet Cong youth were originally from the

South. They were forced by military orders to go North for training, eventually to return to South Viet Nam as infiltrators. Their families, in many cases, still live in villages and hamlets throughout the southern countryside. Many of these young men have also had time to become disillusioned with life under their Communist masters, and the "aggressors" do not seem quite like such fiends when they are seen laughing and playing with and giving candy to children who have known little but hiding and horror.

At its Saigon headquarters, the Psychological Warfare Department of the Vietnamese Armed Forces prepares material for a variety of media. There are posters, leaflets, newspapers, motion pictures, broadcasts, magazines, pamphlets, banners, calendars, booklets, lectures, mobile units, airplanes, loudspeakers—even postcards, stationery, and stage shows. Leaflets and pamphlets are dropped from planes over Viet Cong territory. The objective, obviously, is to point out the advantages of leaving the Communist side.

The Vietnamese Government has established a *"Chieu Hoi"* program for those who decide to abandon the Viet Cong. *Chieu Hoi* means "Open Arms." In addition to the emotional appeal made by this program, very practical material advantages are pointed out, such as the subsidies to be paid upon arrival in the South or after making contact with the nearest program offered.

In comparison with the Communist "program": "No medicine when you are sick," "No support for your family," and "No profession that can guarantee your future," the Nationalist "Open Arms" promise of a warm welcome, money and food for the returnee as well as his family, two suits of clothes, six months' subsidy if he wishes to settle in a New Life (Government-organized) Hamlet, as well as help with vocational training, looks good to men who have spent months in rain-soaked jungles.

From the program's start in February of 1963, it looked good to 11,248 Viet Cong in that year, and in each year since men are abandoning the Viet Cong by the thousands. If a returnee brings a weapon, an additional monetary incentive commensurate with the type of weapon is offered. A pistol will bring a reward of 800 piasters; 1000 for a rifle; 1200 for a foreign-made rifle; 2000 for a submachine gun; 8000 for a 60mm. mortar; 20,000 for a 75mm. recoilless rifle. Officially, the piaster is worth about a penny and a half in United States money.

In startling contrast, no prominent South Vietnamese—politician, educator, writer, artist, military figure, labor leader, or student leader—has ever defected to the Viet Cong. While one million North Vietnamese have fled South to escape the Communist takeover, and some 600,000 South Vietnamese have left areas where Viet Cong influence is strong, no South Vietnamese have voluntarily moved into areas of Viet Cong influence. Also, about 90 per cent of the Government of Viet Nam (GVN) armed forces has *volunteered* to fight the Viet Cong, leaving only 10 per cent as draftees.

Chieu Hoi centers have been set up in every province in South Viet Nam. A National center is located in Saigon, and four regional centers are being established. At the provincial center, the returnee is questioned and then classified according to the status he held in the Viet Cong (military, political agent, sympathizer, etc.).

In addition to his two suits of clothes, the returnee is immediately given 200 piasters for spending money. While he is at the center he receives 18 piasters daily for food. At the small centers the men purchase their own food, but at the large ones there is community buying. During the time they are at the centers—usually sixty days—the men go through "re-orientation" courses. There are no guards, and the men govern themselves. They are given an opportunity for on-the-job training at nearby shops and stores, and in some cases there is vocational training at the center itself.

During my trip to My Tho, I visited the center there, which actually consists of two separate locations. At one, in town, the men are questioned and begin their "re-orientation." At the second place, outside of town, there are clean, well-kept buildings and an adjoining rice farm which the men tend.

Important defectors are taken to Saigon, where their experiences are used for background material for further leaflets, and, also, to evaluate the effectiveness of the program. As men disillusioned with Communism, they are particularly useful in writing letter-leaflets and preparing broadcasts to other Viet Cong, urging them also to join the South.

A typical leaflet prepared by a returnee ran as follows:

To my friends in VC ranks,

I am Le Bay, residing at Phuoc Loc Village, Tuy Phuoc District. I was serving as a liaison agent in VC ranks. . . .

. . . Due to the lack of experience we have been deceived by the VC and become their servants since the day they came to our hamlets. You and I, we have experienced much of hardship, poverty and illtreatment by the VC. Living far from home, from all of my beloved relatives and friends, I was so sorrowful that I finally decided to return when I had an opportunity to do so.

Seeing a Chieu Hoi Open Arms leaflet on June 5, I took four VC carbines and returned to the national cause.

During the days we lived in VC ranks we were

threatened with these words: "If you go back to
the Vietnamese Government, you will be beaten,
tortured and killed." But now I realize that the
truth is far from what they said.

Don't hesitate to return to the national cause.
You will be welcomed and helped to make a living. . . .

The Chieu Hoi doors are wide open. . . .

I hope that you will be able to find a solution
for your life.

> *Binh Dinh Chieu Hoi Center*
> (signed) LE BAY

The average returnee, not writing leaflets or
doing other special work, is given the opportunity
to return to his own hamlet upon completion of
the re-orientation program. That is, if the hamlet
chief and his own family are willing to have him
come back, and also, provided the hamlet is in a
safe area not controlled by the Viet Cong. Most
returnees choose to go back to their former homes.
If, however, his hamlet is in Viet Cong territory,
he can choose another hamlet, again provided he
is acceptable there, or he can go to one of eight
special resettlement hamlets that are now being
built. If he chooses the latter, he is given a 3500-
piaster house and receives a daily allowance of
18 piasters for four months. On leaving the re-
orientation center, the men are given 500 piasters
to help them get started in their new life.

Very few of the men have returned to the Viet Cong, and some who did have defected a second time after their second taste of Communism. One unusual case, particularly gratifying to *Chieu Hoi* officials, involved two Viet Cong who had "defected" and were going through the ordinary re-orientation program. It had such a strong effect that the two men one day shamefacedly admitted they were spies planted by the Viet Cong. Now they were so impressed by the free life in the South that they had decided to join it in earnest. They were permitted to continue with the program.

Thus, through psychological warfare and a special program for defectors, heavy inroads have been made on the ranks of the Viet Cong. Within a three-year period, more than 28,000 men have abandoned the Communist side. This means there are 28,000 fewer terrorists and potential terrorists to harass the people of South Viet Nam.

Civic action and self-help projects provide another answer to terrorism. Basically, this consists of assistance provided by the United States and other Allies in the form of medical care, aid in road building, advice on well digging, transportation of needed materials, and many other services to aid the local population in improving its community life.

Guerrillas invariably need the support or, at least, the nonopposition of local populations to be able to operate effectively. The villager who has received friendly help from the military is unlikely to assist the guerrilla when he appears, and is, in fact, more likely to report his presence to the army.

The money for self-help projects is administered by Vietnamese rural construction budgets; the American Aid Mission assists with funds and technical advice.

The work is done primarily by the technical services of Vietnamese provincial governments, with assistance from Vietnamese Army engineers and, where needed, Allied units.

These projects consist of agricultural assistance, including loans for farm improvement; fertilizer and insecticide distribution; public health and sanitation improvements; as well as the building of schools, market places, and bridges and the paving of roads.

While the greater proportion of assistance has come from the United States, a number of nations are involved. In September, 1964, a 130-man Korean medical unit arrived in Viet Nam to work in a field army hospital. In February, 1965, the Koreans sent a battalion of combat engineers to help build roads, bridges, schools, and dispensaries, and by the fall of 1965 a Division of 15,000 Korean troops, arriving in several contingents, had come to help.

The Australians have sent both military and nonmilitary aid. An eight-man surgical team is working in the Delta province of An Giang, and more teams are expected to arrive soon for work in other provinces. Australian aid to South Viet Nam began in 1956 within the framework of the Colombo Plan. It has contributed technical assistance to improve the water supply and to help with road construction. The Australians donated a 50-kilowatt radio transmitter and such practical materials as corrugated roofing to help refugee resettlement. Many a village and hamlet owes its community radio receiver, which keeps it in touch with life beyond its limited boundaries, to Australian assistance, and the Australians have provided more than one million textbooks for elementary school children in rural Viet Nam.

On the military side, since June, 1962, Australia has sent combat advisors and jungle warfare specialists, as well as an air transport unit. In the latter half of 1965, this nation had increased its military assistance by sending an infantry battalion, a field artillery battery, and support troops totaling 1500 men.

New Zealand first sent a surgical team to Viet Nam in 1963. It has been working in Qui Nhon in Binh Dinh Province. Teaching help at Saigon University has also been provided and 62 scholarships, about half academic and half in technical training. New Zealand's further contributions include a 125-man artillery battery and a 25-man Army engineers detachment.

Despite such help and material support by friendly nations, it is the Vietnamese themselves who have carried the real load in addition to fighting a war. They have been working on soy bean development on experimental farms—an important step toward meeting future nutritional problems. Rural reconstruction has been moving ahead quickly with Vietnamese labor, and roads and bridges are rapidly bringing isolated areas into the mainstream of the country's life.

Here are but a few of the civic action projects undertaken during a typical two-week period in September of 1965:

In Quang Ngai Province, the Vietnamese Army gave plague innoculations to teams consisting of the local Popular Forces. These teams were then sent out to inspect more than 1100 houses for disease-carrying rats and mice, and to check the sanitary conditions in and around the houses.

United States Special Forces doctors conducted a daily sick call at the district dispensary in Loc Ninh District, Binh Long Province. Local inhabitants could have minor injuries treated immediately, and the doctors were also given an opportunity to detect any possible contagious diseases.

Vietnamese Popular Forces in An Giang Province assisted resettlers in clearing homestead areas and erecting dwellings.

In Quan Long District of An Xuyen Province, civic action teams distributed clothing to needy families, as well as books, magazines, and newspapers.

Fifteen hundred mango trees were distributed—approximately 5 to each of 300 families—in Duc Hoa District of Hau Nghia Province.

Thus, the civic action program reaches out to the most remote hamlets in its effort to help the rural folk in the ways they most need help. American Ambassador to Viet Nam, Henry Cabot Lodge, has said: "I think this is a struggle in which air power, sea power, land power all play a decisive part. It's also a struggle in which the civil and the political, the economic and the social, the doctors, the teachers, all play a part. It is a political-military struggle, it's not purely a military struggle, and the military leaders all realize this. You have to take all these different programs and braid them together. . . ."

One of the inevitable tragedies of war is that noncombatant civilians are killed. Artillery fire directed against a town, an air bombing of a hamlet, can undo within minutes all the goodwill painstakingly built up by civic action programs. The problem has been particularly compounded by one of the terror tactics employed by the Viet Cong. They hide in villages and fire on nearby Government or Allied forces, then flee. This leaves the village at the mercy of return fire from the Government troops.

While the Government of Viet Nam wishes to avoid embittering the population by such attacks and making the long-range goal of pacification more difficult, actually, there have been indications that this Viet Cong terror tactic of bringing down fire on a village has backfired. Refugees and Viet Cong defectors have reported that the attitude of the villagers to the Viet Cong has often been: "Why don't they go away and fight elsewhere? Why do they bring the war and destruction to us?"

A directive, based on a similar one to United States commanders, has been issued by the Government of Viet Nam to all Republic of Viet Nam Armed Forces (RVNAF). The directive comments on the nature of the battles which flow back and forth across the homes and fields of innocent inhabitants. It forbids the use of unnecessary force leading to noncombatant casualties in areas temporarily controlled by the Viet Cong.

The directive continues: "The circumstances call for the exercise of restraint more than is normally required of soldiers on the battlefield. Therefore, commanders must strike a balance between the force necessary to accomplish their missions with due regard to the safety of their commands and the high importance of reducing to a minimum casualties inflicted on the non-combatant populace."

Guidelines were set for commanders. Without quoting the directive in its entire length and detail, some of the more important instructions from the United States directive follow:

"Commanders will consider the military and psychological objectives of each operation.

"Troop indoctrination briefings will be held before each operation to emphasize the short- and long-range importance of minimizing non-combatant casualties.

"The proper selection of landing zones, the careful planning and execution of air strikes, and the proper employment of artillery and armed helicopters will avoid unnecessary damage to lives and property of non-combatants.

"Forward air controllers and armed helicopter commanders will be briefed on areas to be avoided because of the presence of friendly or potentially friendly population.

"With due regard to security and success of the mission . . . the people will be warned of impending air strikes or operations by leaflets and broadcasts.

"A civic action plan should be developed to support each operation . . . [especially] if the area has been controlled by the VC.

"Operations should be planned in coordination with province and district chiefs with due regard to the security of plans. . . .

"Assignment to U. S. combat forces of qualified Vietnamese Armed Forces liaison officers is essential. . . . These liaison officers can assist in identification of friend or foe and can help to insure close coordination with all Vietnamese forces. . . .

"Established rules of good military conduct and discipline must be enforced.

" 'U. S. forces are establishing the reputation of being able to move at will throughout South Vietnam and are defeating VC forces encountered.' This reputation is producing innumerable psychological benefits and is hastening the end of the war. Therefore, these same forces must constantly demonstrate their concern for the safety of non-combatants—their compassion for the injured—their willingness to aid and assist the sick, the hungry, and the displaced. [Although this guideline is taken directly from the United States instructions to its own troops, the Government of Viet Nam has recognized the value of its application to Vietnamese troops.]

"Emphasis is placed on the employment of psywar [psychological warfare] technique. A Psywar/Civic Action plan will be prepared to support each operation. Separation of non-combatants from the VC by leaflets, loudspeakers, and/or face-to-face teams is to be accomplished whenever possible. . . ."

Separation of noncombatants from the Viet Cong—this is a primary goal of the Allied and South Vietnamese forces, not only in a physical sense, but in an ideological sense as well. The Viet

Cong attempt to gain control through terror. The Allies seek to win the support of the populace through civic action programs that will free them from terror. This, in fine, is the nonmilitary conflict.

A few years ago, in an effort to counter attacks on isolated villages, a former South Vietnamese regime attempted to adopt a system successfully employed by the British when they fought Communist guerrillas in Malaya: the setting up of "strategic hamlets." These hamlets were heavily fortified and guarded by troops, and all citizens in the areas were required to live in them. The system did not work in Viet Nam, however, primarily because the people resented and resisted being uprooted from their farms and their ancestral graves.

Now a different rural defensive system has been developed and is being expanded. In addition to the regular Vietnamese Army, two other military organizations are operational. Regional Forces are set up in the provinces. They generally operate only within their own provinces, but are nearly as well equipped and trained as the regular troops. At a lesser military level are the Popular Forces. Popular Forces units are established in the villages, are required only to defend their own villages and are not subject to transfer elsewhere.

Training and equipment of the Popular Forces is minimal. However, the Popular Forces often bear the brunt of Viet Cong attacks, because they are the only defensive force many hamlets and villages have. A hamlet is usually guarded by a squad of from 8 to 12 men. A village has a platoon of 30 to 50 men. And a district town (capital) generally has one or two companies of Popular Forces, with 150 men in each company.

Although the idea of strategic hamlets has been discarded, a new concept is being developed which appears to be more successful: the establishment of "New Life Hamlets." Basically, this consists of greater central government control over existing hamlets and better organization of their defenses. A census is taken and identification cards are issued to all residents. If the hamlet has no chief, one is appointed. Political officers move in and give the hamlet political orientation (i.e., pro-government and anti-Viet Cong).

A watchtower is built and manned so that proper warning can be given of a Viet Cong attack. Some sort of shelter is built in each house, so the occupants can hide in the event of an attack. Barbed wire is set up around the hamlet, and a Popular Forces squad is organized, trained, and equipped. The hamlet now has a better chance to defend itself, and it is more firmly under the government's protection.

In urban areas, especially Saigon, the problem is vastly different. Saigon is a sprawling city with a population of some two million people, and it is not an easy task for the police to protect the

citizenry from the secret terrorists who strike swift-
ly, then flee to hide amid the population. One major problem is that the Saigon uniformed police
force consists of only 10,000 men, far below what
is needed. Of these, half are doing clerical work
and stationary guard duty, and only 5000 remain
for patrol and other operational tasks. To help
remedy this situation caused mainly by a manpower shortage, the Government is increasing efforts to add to the size of the police organization.

Several Vietnamese police and intelligence di-
visions are involved in opposing Viet Cong terrorism. These include the Vietnamese Central
Intelligence Organization, the Military Security
Service, and two branches of the National Police,
the Judicial Police and the Special Branch. The
Special Branch, a plainclothes department, is most
directly involved in counter measures against
terrorism.

American participation is primarily concerned
with advising and assisting the Vietnamese authorities, and protecting American nationals and in-
stallations.

There are many phases to the Vietnamese terror-
blocking program in the cities. The following are
among the more important steps that have been
taken:

1. "Resources control," i.e., cutting off Viet Cong
resources and movements. At roads leading into
Saigon, police at checkpoints search vehicles to

make sure that explosives are not being smuggled into the city. In the city itself, white-uniformed police on various streets spot-check passing cars: for example, every fifth or every tenth car is stopped and searched, and its occupants asked to show identification papers. A census is conducted frequently in an effort to keep track of the persons living in an area; an unexplained "cousin" from the interior would be suspect as a possible Viet Cong.

2. There are nine precincts in Saigon, and in eeach one a "sweep" is carried out nightly. The police block off an area, then examine every square foot of it, seeking Viet Cong, criminals, and anyone else caught in the net. Depending on the size of the area being searched, anywhere from 50 to 1000 police participate, and in at least one case 1400 police were used.

3. The Saigon police utilize routine police intelligence techniques. They get tips from informants, they give out rewards, and they have occasionally succeeded in penetrating the Viet Cong apparatus with their own spies.

4. Normal police investigative techniques are used.

5. Physical security is maintained at key places, such as police stations, government buildings, military posts, and so on. Barbed wire is strung, the number of guards is increased, the backgrounds of civilian personnel are carefully checked, and

persons entering the buildings must identify themselves.

6. Vehicles driving into the compounds of buildings are searched. A device that has been developed is a mirror attached to a stick. This is passed along the underside of the car to reveal any explosives concealed underneath.

7. Because of the Viet Cong penchant for driving explosive-laden vehicles close to target buildings, the streets around United States diplomatic buildings are blocked by sections of sewer pipe, upended and filled with concrete to make heavy, effective barriers. Security at key buildings around the city is constantly checked by radio-equipped cars.

That this program is increasingly effective is demonstrated by the fact that about a thousand persons are apprehended weekly; among these usually about twenty Viet Cong are caught, plus an average of ten more persons who are highly suspect. Viet Cong weapons are also being unearthed at an average of twenty grenades and five pistols per month. In one raid in October, 1965, the police arrested five men and three women and found twenty-five grenades, five of which were Russian.

When the terror and subversion have been halted, what lies ahead for South Viet Nam?

Once the Viet Cong have been pushed back,

political stability will become possible for South Viet Nam. It can choose its own government and manage its own affairs in accordance with its own wishes.

Economically, the prospects for the country are very good. It is a rich, fertile land with a talented, hard-working population. It can feed itself and create a healthy economy with the products of its labor.

Sociologically, Viet Nam's leaders are prepared to carry out a peaceful revolution—giving every man his voice in the country's affairs. Land reforms can be put into effect which will permit farmers to own the land on which they toil and to gain the benefits of the crops they raise. In fact, social reforms in many directions are already under way.

While all of this will take time, once the subversion and terror have ended, the future can be devoted to hard work, and then South Viet Nam can take her place among the Free Nations of the world.